The Game of Life and I

Your Invisible Power and

How to Live Life and Love it,

(3 Power Books)

Florence Scovel Shinn and Genevieve Behrend

CONTENTS

BOOK ONE

THE GAME OF LIFE AND HOW TO PLAY IT

FLORENCE SCOVEL SHINN

1

THE GAME

Most people consider life a battle, but it is not a battle, it is a game.

It is a game, however, which cannot be played successfully without the knowledge of spiritual law, and the Old and the New Testaments give the rules of the game with wonderful clearness. Jesus Christ taught that it was a great game of *Giving and Receiving.*

"Whatsoever a man soweth that shall he also reap." This means that whatever man sends out in word or deed, will return to him; what he gives, he will receive.

If he gives hate, he will receive hate; if he gives love, he will receive love; if he gives criticism, he will receive criticism; if he lies he will be lied to; if he cheats he will be cheated. We are taught also, that the imaging faculty plays a leading part in the game of life.

"Keep thy heart (or imagination) with all diligence, for out of it are the issues of life." (Prov. 4:23.) This means that what man images, sooner or later externalizes in his affairs, I know of a man who feared a certain disease. It was a very rare disease and difficult to get, but he pictured it continually and read about it until it manifested in his body, and he died, the victim of distorted imagination.

So we see, to play successfully the game of life, we must train the imaging faculty. A person with an imaging faculty trained to image only good, brings into his life "every righteous desire of his heart" - health, wealth, love, friends, perfect self-expression, his highest ideals.

The imagination has been called, "The Scissors of The Mind," and it is ever cutting, cutting, day by day, the pictures man sees there, and sooner or later he meets his own creations in his outer world. To train the imagination successfully, man must understand the workings of his mind. The Greeks said: "Know Thyself."

There are three departments of the mind, the *subconscious, conscious and superconscious.* The subconscious, is simply power, without direction. It is like steam or electricity, and it does what it is directed to do; it has no power of induction.

Whatever man feels deeply or images clearly, is impressed upon the subconscious mind, and carried out in minutest detail.

For example: a woman I know, when a child, always "made believe" she was a widow. She "dressed up" in black clothes and wore a long black veil, and people thought she was very clever and amusing. She grew up and married a man with whom she was deeply in love. In a short time he died and she wore black and a sweeping veil for many years. The picture of herself as a widow was impressed upon the subconscious mind, and in due time worked itself out, regardless of the havoc created.

The conscious mind has been called mortal or carnal mind. It is the human mind and sees life as it *appears to be.* It sees death, disaster, sickness, poverty and limitation of every kind, and it impresses the subconscious. The **superconscious** mind is the God Mind within each man, and is the realm of perfect ideas.

In it, is the *"perfect pattern"* spoken of by Plato, **The Divine Design**; for there is a **Divine Design** for each person.

"There is a place that you are to fill and no one else can fill, something you are to do, which no one else can do." There is a perfect picture of this in the **superconscious mind.** It usually flashes across the conscious as an unattainable ideal - "something too good to be true." In reality it is man's true destiny (or destination) flashed to him from the Infinite Intelligence which is *within himself.* Many people, however, are in ignorance of their true destinies and are striving for things and situations which do not belong to them, and would only bring failure and dissatisfaction if attained.

For example: A woman came to me and asked me to "speak the word" that she would marry a certain man with whom she was very much in love. (She called him A. B.)

I replied that this would be a violation of spiritual law, but that I would speak the word for the right man, the "divine selection," the man who belonged to her by divine right.

I added, "If A. B. is the right man you can't lose him, and if he isn't, you will receive his equivalent." She saw A. B. frequently but no headway was made in their friendship. One evening she called, and said, "Do you know, for the last week, A. B. hasn't seemed so wonderful to me." I replied, "Maybe he is not the divine selection - another man may be the right one." Soon after that, she met another man who fell in love with her at once, and who said she was his ideal. In fact, he said all the things that she had always wished A. B. would say to her.

She remarked, "It was quite uncanny."

She soon returned his love, and lost all interest in A. B. This shows the law of substitution. A right idea was substituted for a wrong one, therefore there was no loss or sacrifice involved.

Jesus Christ said, "Seek ye first the kingdom of God and his righteousness; and all these things shall be added unto you," and he said the Kingdom *was within man.*

The Kingdom is the realm of *right ideas,* or the divine pattern.

Jesus Christ taught that man's words played a leading part in the game of life. "By your words ye are justified and by your words ye are condemned."

Many people have brought disaster into their lives through idle words.

For example: A woman once asked me why her life was now one of poverty of limitation. Formerly she had a home, was surrounded by beautiful things and had often tired of the management of her home, and had said repeatedly, "I'm sick and tired of things - I wish I lived in a trunk," and she added: "Today I am living in that trunk." She had spoken herself into a trunk. The subconscious mind has no sense of humor and people often joke themselves into unhappy experiences.

For example: A woman who had a great deal of money, joked continually about "getting ready for the poorhouse." In a few years she was almost destitute, having impressed the subconscious mind with a picture of lack and limitation. Fortunately the law works both ways, and a situation of lack may be changed to one of plenty.

For example: A woman came to me one hot summer's day for a "treatment" for prosperity. She was worn out, dejected and discouraged. She said she possessed just eight dollars in the world. I said, "Good, we'll bless the eight dollars and multiply them as Jesus Christ multiplied the loaves and fishes," for He taught that **every man** had the power to bless and to multiply, to heal and to prosper. She said, "What shall I do next?"

I replied, "Follow intuition. Have you a 'hunch' to do anything, or to go anywhere?" Intuition means, intuition, or to be taught from within. It is man's unerring guide, and I will deal more fully with its laws in a following chapter. The woman replied: "I don't know - I seem to have a 'hunch' to go home; I've just enough money for carfare." Her home was in a distant city and was one of lack and limitation, and the reasoning mind (or intellect) would have said: "Stay in New York and get work and make some money." I replied, "Then go home - never violate a hunch." I spoke the following words for her: **Infinite Spirit open the way for great abundance for --. She is an irresistible magnet for all that belongs to her by divine right."** I told her to repeat it continually also. She left for home immediately. In calling on a woman one day, she linked up with an old friend of her family.

Through this friend, she received thousands of dollars in a most miraculous way. She has said to me often, "Tell people about the woman who came to you with eight dollars and a hunch."

There is always **plenty on man's pathway;** but it can only be **brought into manifestation** through desire, faith or the spoken word. Jesus Christ brought out clearly that man must make the **first move.**

"**Ask,** and it shall be given you, seek, and ye shall find, knock, and it shall be opened unto you. (Mat. 7:7).

In the scriptures we read:

"Concerning the works of my hands, command ye me." Infinite Intelligence, God, is ever ready to carry out man's smallest or greatest demands.

Every desire, uttered or unexpressed, is a demand. We are often startled by having a wish suddenly fulfilled.

For example: One Easter, having seen many beautiful rose-trees in the florists' windows, I wished I would receive one, and for an instant saw it mentally being carried in the door. Easter came, and with it a beautiful rose-tree. I thanked my friend the following day, and told her it was just what I had wanted.

'She replied, "I didn't send you a rose-tree, I sent you lilies!"

"The man had mixed the order, and sent me a rose-tree simply because I had started the law in action, and *I had to have a rose-tree.*

Nothing stands between man and his highest ideals and every desire of his heart, but doubt and fear. When man can "wish without worrying," every desire will be instantly fulfilled.

I will explain more fully in a following chapter the scientific reason for this and fear must be erased from the consciousness. It is man's only enemy - fear of lack, fear of failure, fear of sickness, fear of loss and a feeling of *insecurity on some plane.* Jesus Christ said: "Why are ye fearful, oh ye of little faith?" (Mat. 8:26) So we can see we must substitute faith for fear, for fear is only inverted faith; it is faith in evil instead of good.

The object of the game of life is to see clearly one's good and to obliterate all mental pictures of evil. This must be done by impressing the subconscious mind with a realization of good. A very brilliant man, who has attained great success, told me he had suddenly erased all fear from his consciousness by reading a sign which hung in a room. He saw printed, in large letters this statement - *Why worry, it will probably never happen."* These words were stamped indelibly upon his subconscious mind, and he has now a firm conviction that only good can come into his life, therefore only *good can manifest.*

In the following chapter I will deal with the different methods of impressing the subconscious mind. It is man's faithful servant but one must be careful to give it the right orders. Man has ever a silent listener at his side - his subconscious mind.

Every thought, every word is impressed upon it and carried out in amazing detail. It is like a singer making a record on the sensitive disc of the phonographic plate. Every note and tone of the singer's voice is registered. If he coughs or hesitates, it is registered also. So let us break all the old bad records in the subconscious mind, the records of our lives which we do not wish to keep, and make new and beautiful ones.

Speak these words aloud, with power and conviction: "I now smash and demolish (by my spoken word) every untrue record in my subconscious mind. They shall return to the dust-heap of their native nothingness, for they came from my own vain imaginings. I now make my perfect records through the Christ within - The records of *Health, Wealth, Love and perfect self-Expression."* This is the square of life, *The Game completed.*

In the following chapters, I will show how man can **change** his **conditions by changing his words.** Any man who does not know the power of the word, is behind the times.

"Death and Life are in the power of the tongue." (Prov. 18:21.)

2
THE LAW OF PROSPERITY

One of the greatest messages given to the race through the scriptures is that God is man's supply and that man can release, *through his spoken word,* all that belongs to him by divine right. He must, however, have *perfect faith in his spoken word.*

Isaiah said, "My word shall not return unto me void, but shall accomplish that where it is sent." We know now, that words and thoughts are a tremendous vibratory force, ever moulding man's body and affairs.

A woman came to me in great distress and said she was to be sued on the fifteenth of the month for three thousand dollars. She knew no way of getting the money and was in despair.

I told her God was her supply, and *that there is a supply for every demand.*

So I spoke the word! I gave thanks that the woman would receive three thousand dollars at the right time in the right way. I told her she must have perfect faith, and act her *perfect faith*. The fifteenth came but no money had materialized.

She called me on the 'phone and asked what she was to do. I replied, "It is Saturday, so they won't sue you today, Your part is to act rich, thereby showing perfect faith that you will receive it by Monday." She asked me to lunch with her to keep up her courage. When I joined her at a restaurant, I said, "This is no time to economize. Order an expensive luncheon, act as if you have already received the three thousand dollars."

"All things whatsoever ye ask in prayer, *believing,* ye shall receive." "You must act as if you *had already received."* The next morning she called me on the 'phone and asked me to stay with her during the day, I said "No, you are divinely protected and God is never too late."

In the evening she 'phoned again, greatly excited and said, "My dear, a miracle has happened! I was sitting in my room this morning, when the doorbell rang, I said to the maid: 'Don't let anyone in.' The maid however, looked out the window and said, 'It's your cousin with the long white beard.'

So I said, 'Call him back. I would like to see him.' He was just turning the corner, when he heard the maid's voice, and he came back.

He talked for about an hour, and just as he was leaving he said, 'Oh, by the way, how are finances?'

I told him I needed the money, and he said, 'Why, my dear, I will give you three thousand dollars the first of the month. I didn't like to tell him I was going to be sued. What shall I do? I won't receive it till the first of the month, and I must have it tomorrow." I said, "I'll keep on 'treating.'"

I said, "Spirit is never too late. I give thanks she has received the money on the invisible plane and that it manifests on time." The next morning her cousin called her up and said, "Come to my office this morning and I will give you the money." That afternoon, she had three thousand dollars to her credit in the bank, and wrote checks as rapidly as her excitement would permit.

If one asks for success and prepares for failure, he will get the situation he has prepared for. For example: A man came to me asking me to speak the word that a certain debt would be wiped out.

I found he spent his time planning what he would say to the man when he did not pay his bill, thereby neutralizing my words. He should have seen himself paying the debt. We have a wonderful illustration of this in the bible, relating to the three kings who were in the desert, without water for their men and horses. They consulted the prophet Elisha, who gave them this astonishing message: "Thus saith the Lord - Ye shall not see wind, neither shall ye see rain, yet make this valley full of ditches." Man must prepare for the thing he has asked for, **when there isn't the slightest sign of it in sight.**

For example: A woman found it necessary to look for an apartment during the year when there was a great shortage of apartments in New York. It was considered almost an impossibility, and her friends were sorry for her and said, "Isn't it too bad, you'll have to store your furniture and live in a hotel." She replied, **"You needn't feel sorry for me, I'm a superman, and I'll get an apartment."**

She spoke the words: **"Infinite Spirit, open the way for the right apartment."** She knew there was a supply for every demand, and that she was "unconditioned," working on the spiritual plane, and that "one with God is a majority." She had contemplated buying new blankets, when the "tempter," the adverse thought or reasoning mind, suggested, "Don't buy the blankets, perhaps, after all, you won't get an apartment and you will have no use for them." She promptly replied (to herself): "I'll dig my ditches by buying the blankets!" So she prepared for the apartment - acted as though she already had it.

She found one in a miraculous way, and it was given to her although there were over **two hundred other applicants.**

The blankets showed active faith.

It is needless to say that the ditches dug by the three kings in the desert were filled to over-flowing. (Read, II Kings) Getting into the spiritual swing of things is no easy matter for the average person. The adverse thoughts of doubt and fear surge from the subconscious. They are the "army of the aliens" which must be put to flight. This explains why it is so often, "darkest before the dawn."

A big demonstration is usually preceded by tormenting thoughts.

Having made a statement of high spiritual truth one challenges the old beliefs in the subconscious, and "error is exposed" to be put out.

This is the time when one must make his affirmations of truth repeatedly, and rejoice and give thanks that he has already received, "Before ye call I shall answer." This means that "every good and perfect gift" is already man's awaiting his recognition.

Man can only receive what he sees himself receiving.

The children of Israel were told that they could have all the land they could see. This is true of every man. He has only the land within his own mental vision. Every great work, every big accomplishment, has been brought into manifestation through holding to the vision, and often just before the big achievement, comes apparent failure and discouragement.

The children of Israel when they reached the "Promised Land," were afraid to go in, for they said it was filled with giants who made them feel like grasshoppers. "And there we saw the giants and we were in our own sight as grasshoppers." This is almost every man's experience. However, the one who knows spiritual law, is undisturbed by appearance, and rejoices while he is "yet in captivity." That is, he holds to his vision and gives thanks that the end is accomplished, he has received.

Jesus Christ gave a wonderful example of this. He said to his disciples: "Say not ye, there are yet four months and then cometh the harvest? Behold, I say unto you, lift up your eyes and look on the fields; for they are ripe already to harvest." His clear vision pierced the "world of matter" and he saw clearly the fourth dimensional world, things as they really are, perfect and complete in Divine Mind. So man must ever hold the vision of his journey's end and demand the manifestation of that which he has already received. It may be his perfect, health, love, supply, self-expression, home or friends.

They are all finished and perfect ideas registered in Divine Mind (man's own superconscious mind) and must come through him, not to him.

For example: A man came to me asking for treatments for success. It was imperative that he raise, within a certain, fifty-thousand dollars for his business. The time limit was almost up, when he came to me in despair. No one wanted to invest in his enterprise, and the bank had flatly refused a loan.

I replied: "I suppose you lost your temper while at the bank, therefore your power. You can control any situation if you first control yourself."

"Go back to the bank," I added, "and I will treat." My treatment was: "You are identified in love with the spirit of everyone connected with the bank. Let the divine idea come out of this situation."

He replied, "Woman, you are talking about an impossibility. Tomorrow is Saturday; the bank closes at twelve, and my train won't get me there until ten, and the time limit is up tomorrow, and anyway they won't do it. It's too late."

I replied, "God doesn't need any time and is never too late. With Him all things are possible." I added, "I don't know anything about business, but I know all about God." He replied: "It all sounds fine when I sit here listening to you, but when I go out it's terrible."

He lived in a distant city, and I did not hear from him for a week, then came a letter. It read: "You were right. I raised the money, and will never again doubt the truth of all that you told me."

I saw him a few weeks later, and I said, "what happened?

You evidently had plenty of time, after all." He replied, "My train was late, and I got there just fifteen minutes to twelve. I walked into the bank quietly and said, 'I have come for the loan,' and they gave it to me without a question."

It was the last fifteen minutes of the time allotted to him, and Infinite Spirit was not too late. In this instance the man could never have demonstrated alone. He needed someone to help him hold to the vision. This is what one man can do for another.

Jesus Christ knew the truth of this when he said: "If two of you shall agree on earth as touching anything that they shall ask, it shall be done for them of my Father which is in heaven." One gets too close to his own affairs and becomes doubtful and fearful.

The friend or "healer" sees clearly the success, health, or prosperity, and never wavers, because he is not close to the situation.

It is much easier to "demonstrate" for someone else than for one's self, so a person should not hesitate to ask for help, if he feels himself wavering.

A keen observer of life once said, "no man can fail, if some one person sees him successful." Such is the power of the vision, and many a great man owed his success to a wife, or sister, or a friend who "believed in him" and held without wavering to the perfect pattern!

3
THE POWER OF THE WORD

A person knowing the power of the word, becomes very careful of his conversation. He has only to watch the reaction of his words to know that they do "not return void." Through his spoken word, man is continually making laws for himself.

I knew a man who said, "I always miss a car. It invariably pulls out just as I arrive."

His daughter said: "I always catch a car. It's sure to come just as I get there." This occurred for years. Each had made a separate law for himself, one of failure, one of success.. This is the psychology of superstitions.

The horse-shoe or rabbit's foot contains no power, but man's spoken word and belief that it will bring good luck creates expectancy in the subconscious mind, and attracts a "lucky situation." I find however, this will not "work" when man has advanced spiritually and knows a higher law. One cannot turn back, and must put away "graven images." For example: Two men in my class had had great success in business for several months, when suddenly everything "went to smash." We tried to analyze the situation, and I found, instead of making their affirmations and looking to God for success and prosperity, they had each bought a "lucky monkey." I said: "Oh I see, you have been trusting in the lucky monkeys instead of God." "Put away the lucky monkeys and call on the law of forgiveness," for man has power to forgive or neutralize his mistakes.

They decided to throw the lucky monkeys down a coalhole, and all went well again. This does not mean, however, that one should throw away every "lucky" ornament or horseshoe about the house, but he must recognize that the power back of it is the one and only power, God, and that the object simply gives him a feeling of expectancy.

I was with a friend, one day, who was in deep despair. In crossing the street, she picked up a horse-shoe. Immediately, she was filled with joy and hope. She said God had sent her the horseshoe in order to keep up her courage.

It was indeed, at that moment, about the only thing that could have registered in her consciousness. Her hope became faith, and she ultimately made a wonderful demonstration. I wish to make the point clear that the men previously mentioned were depending on the monkeys, alone, while this woman recognized the power back of the horseshoe.

I know, in my own case, it took a long while to get out of a belief that a certain thing brought disappointment. If the thing happened, disappointment invariably followed. I found the only way I could make a change in the subconscious, was by asserting, "There are not two powers, there is only one power, God, therefore, there are not disappointments, and this thing means a happy surprise." I noticed a change at once, and happy surprises commenced coming my way.

I have a friend who said nothing could induce her to walk under a ladder. I said, "If you are afraid, you are giving in to a belief in two powers, Good and Evil, instead of one. As God is absolute, there can be no opposing power, unless man makes the false of evil for himself. To show you believe in only One Power, God, and that there is no power or reality in evil, walk under the next ladder you see." Soon after, she went to her bank. She wished to open her box in the safe-deposit vault, and there stood a ladder on her pathway. It was impossible to reach the box without passing under the ladder. She quailed with fear and turned back. She could not face the lion on her pathway. However, when she reached the street, my words rang in her ears and she decided to return and walk under it. It was a big moment in her life, for ladders had held her in bondage for years. She retraced her steps to the vault, and the ladder was no longer there! This so often happens! If one is willing to do a thing he is afraid to do, he does not have to.

It is the law of nonresistance, which is so little understood.

Someone has said that courage contains genius and magic. Face a situation fearlessly, and there is no situation to face; it falls away of its own weight.

The explanation is, that fear attracted the ladder on the woman's pathway, and fearlessness removed it.

Thus the invisible forces are ever working for man who is always "pulling the strings" himself, though he does not know it. Owing to the vibratory power of words, whatever man voices, he begins to attract. People who continually speak of disease, invariably attract it.

After man knows the truth, he cannot be too careful of his words. For example: I have a friend who often says on the 'phone, "Do come to see me and have an old-fashioned chat." This "old-fashioned chat" means an hour of about five hundred to a thousand destructive words, the principal topics being loss, lack, failure and sickness.

I reply: "No, I thank you. I've had enough old-fashioned chats in my life, they are too expensive, but I will be glad to have a new-fashioned chat, and talk about what we want, not what we don't want." There is an old saying that man only dares use his words for three purposes, to "heal, bless or prosper." What man says of others will be said of him, and what he wishes for another, he is wishing for himself. "Curses, like chickens, come home to roost."

If a man wishes someone "bad luck," he is sure to attract bad luck himself. If he wishes to aid someone to success, he is wishing and aiding himself to success.

The body may be renewed and transformed through the spoken word and clear vision, and disease be completely wiped out of the consciousness. The metaphysician knows that all disease has a mental correspondence, and in order to heal the body one must first "heal the soul."

The soul is the subconscious mind, and it must be "saved" from wrong thinking.

In the twenty-third psalm, we read: "He restoreth my soul." This means that the subconscious mind or soul, must be restored with the right ideas, and the "mystical marriage" is the marriage of the soul and the spirit, or the subconscious and superconscious mind. They must be one. When the subconscious is flooded with the perfect ideas of the superconscious, God and man are one, "I and the Father are one." That is, he is one with the realm of perfect ideas; he is the man made in God's likeness and image (imagination) and is given power and dominion over all created things, his mind, body and affairs.

It is safe to say that all sickness and unhappiness come from the violation of the law of love. A new commandment I give unto you, "Love one another," and in the Game of Life, love or good-will takes every trick.

For example: A woman I know, had, for years an appearance of a terrible skin disease. The doctors told her it was incurable, and she was in despair. she was on the stage, and she feared she would soon have to give up her profession, and she had no other means of support. She, however, procured a good engagement, and on the opening night, made a great "hit." She received flattering notices from the critics, and was joyful and elated. The next day she received a notice of dismissal. A man in the cast had been jealous of her success and had caused her to be sent away. She felt hatred and resentment taking complete possession of her, and she cried out, "Oh God don't let me hate that man." That night she worked for hours "in the silence."

She said, "I soon came into a very deep silence. I seemed to be at peace with myself, with the man, and with the whole world. I continued this for two following nights, and on the third day I found I was healed completely of the skin disease!" In asking for love, or good will, she had fulfilled the law, ("for love is the fulfilling of the law") and the disease (which came from subconscious resentment) was wiped out.

Continual criticism produces rheumatism, as critical, inharmonious thoughts cause unnatural deposits in the blood, which settle in the joints.

False growths are caused by jealousy, hatred unforgiveness, fear, etc. Every disease is caused by a mind not at ease. I said once, in my class, "There is no use asking anyone 'What's the matter with you?' we might just as well say, 'Who's the matter with you?' "Unforgiveness is the most prolific cause of disease. It will harden arteries or liver, and affect the eye-sight. In its train are endless ills. I called on a woman, one day, who said she was ill from having eaten a poisoned oyster. I replied, "Oh, no, the oyster was harmless, you poisoned the oyster. What's the matter with you?" She answered, "Oh about nineteen people." She had quarreled with nineteen people and had become so inharmonious that she attracted the wrong oyster.

Any inharmony on the external, indicates there is mental inharmony. "As the within, so the without."

Man's only enemies are within himself. "And a man's foes shall be they of his own household." Personality is one of the last enemies to be overcome, as this planet is taking its initiation in love. It was Christ's message - "Peace on Earth, good will towards man." The enlightened man, therefore, endeavors to perfect himself upon his neighbor. His work is with himself, to send out goodwill and blessings to every man, and the marvelous thing is, that if one blesses a man he has no power to harm him.

For example: A man came to me asking to "treat" for success in business. He was selling machinery, and rival appeared on the scene with what he proclaimed, was a better machine, and my friend feared defeat. I said, "First of all, we must wipe out all fear, and know that God protects your interest, and that the divine idea must come out of the situation. That is, the right machine will be sold, by the right man, to the right man." And I added, "Don't hold one critical thought towards that man. Bless him all day, and be willing not to sell your machine, if it isn't the divine idea." So he went to the meeting, fearless and nonresistant, and blessing the other man. He said the outcome was very remarkable. the other man's machine refused to work, and he sold his without the slightest difficulty. "But I say unto you, love your enemies, bless them that curse you, do good to them that hate you, and pray for them which spitefully use you and persecute you."

"Good-will produces a great aura of protection about the one who sends it, and "No weapon that is formed against him shall prosper." In other words, love and good-will destroy the enemies with one's self, therefore, one has no enemies on the external!

"There is peace on earth for him who sends good-will to man!"

4
THE LAW OF NONRESISTANCE

Nothing on earth can resist an absolutely nonresistant person.

The Chinese say that water is the most powerful element, because it is perfectly nonresistant. It can wear away a rock, and sweep all before it.

Jesus Christ said, "Resist not evil," for He knew in reality, there is no evil, therefore nothing to resist. Evil has come of man's "vain imagination," or a belief in two powers, good and evil.

There is an old legend, that Adam and Eve ate of "Maya the Tree of Illusion," and saw two powers instead of one power, God.

Therefore, evil is a false law man has made for himself, through psychoma or soul sleep. Soul sleep means, that man's soul has been hypnotized by the race belief (of sin, sickness and death, etc.) which is carnal or mortal thought, and his affairs have out-pictured his illusions.

We have read in a preceding chapter, that man's soul is his subconscious mind, and whatever he feels deeply, good or bad, is outpictured by that faithful servant. His body and affairs show forth what he has been picturing. The sick man has pictured sickness, the poor man, poverty, the rich man, wealth.

People often say, "why does a little child attract illness, when it is too young even to know what it means?" I answer that children are sensitive and receptive to the thoughts of others about them, and often outpicture the fears of their parents.

I heard a metaphysician once say, "If you do not run your subconscious mind yourself, someone else will run it for you."

Mothers often, unconsciously, attract illness and disaster to their children, by continually holding them in thoughts of fear, and watching for symptoms.

For example: A friend asked a woman if her little girl had had the measles. She replied promptly, "not yet!" This implied that she was expecting the illness, and therefore, preparing the way for what she did not want for herself and child.

However, the man who is centered and established in right thinking, the man who sends out only good-will to his fellow-man, and who is without fear, cannot be **touched or influenced by the negative thoughts of others.** In fact, he could then receive only good thoughts, as he himself, sends forth only thoughts.

Resistance is Hell, for it places man in a "state of torment." A metaphysician once gave me a wonderful recipe for taking every trick in the game of life, it is the acme of nonresistance. He gave it in this way: "At one time in my life, I baptized children, and of course, they had many names. Now I no longer baptize children, but I baptize events, but ***I give every event the***

same name. If I have a failure I baptize it success, in the name of the Father, and of the Son, and of the Holy Ghost!"

In this, we see the great law of transmutation, founded on nonresistance. Through his spoken word, every failure was transmuted into success.

For example: A woman who required money, and who knew the spiritual law of opulence, was thrown continually in a business-way, with a man who made her feel very poor. He talked lack and limitation and she commenced to catch his poverty thoughts, so she disliked him, and blamed him for her failure. She knew in order to demonstrate her supply, she must first feel that she **had received - a feeling of opulence must precede its manifestation.**

It dawned on her, one day, that she was resisting the situation, and seeing two powers instead of one. So she blessed the man and baptized the situation "Success"! She affirmed, "As there is only one power, God, this man is here for my good and my prosperity" (just what he did not seem to be there for). Soon after that she met, **through this man,** a woman who gave her for a service rendered, several thousand dollars, and the man moved to a distant city, and faded harmoniously from her life. Make the statement, "Every man is a golden link in the chain of my good," for all men are God in manifestation, **awaiting the opportunity given by man, himself, to serve the divine plan of his life.** "Bless your enemy, and you rob him of his ammunition." His arrows will be transmuted into blessings.

This law is true of nations as well as individuals. Bless a nation, send love and good-will to every inhabitant and it is robbed of its power to harm.

Man can only get the right idea of nonresistance, through spiritual understanding. My students have often said: "I don't want to be a door-mat." I reply "when you use nonresistance with wisdom, no one will ever be able to walk over you."

Another example: One day I was impatiently awaiting an important telephone call. I resisted every call that came in and made no out-going calls myself, reasoning that it might interfere with the one I was awaiting.

Instead of saying, "Divine ideas never conflict, the call will come at the right time," leaving it to Infinite Intelligence to arrange, I commenced to manage things myself - I made the battle mine, not God's and remained tense and anxious. The bell did not ring for about an hour, and I glanced at the 'phone and found the receiver had been off that length of time, and the 'phone was disconnected. My anxiety, fear and belief in interference, had brought on a total eclipse of the telephone. Realizing what I had done, I commenced blessing the situation at once; I baptized it "success," and affirmed, "I cannot lose any call that belongs to me by divine right; I am under **grace, and not under law.**"

A friend rushed out to the nearest telephone, to notify the Company to reconnect.

She entered a crowded grocery, but the proprietor left his customers and attended to the call himself. My 'phone was connected at once, and two minutes later, I received a very important call, and about an hour afterward, the one I had been awaiting.

One's ships come in over a calm sea.

So long as man resists a situation, he will have it with him. If he runs away from it, it will run after him.

For example: I repeated this to a woman one day, and she replied, "How true that is! I was unhappy at home, I disliked my mother, who was critical and domineering; so I ran away and was married - but I married my mother, for my husband was exactly like my mother, and I had the same situation to face again." "Agree with thine adversary quickly."

This means, agree that the adverse situation is good, be undisturbed by it, and it falls away of its own weight. "None of these things move me," is a wonderful affirmation.

The inharmonious situation comes from some inharmony within man himself.

When there is, in him, no emotional response to an inharmonious situation, it fades away forever, from his pathway.

So we see man's work is ever with himself.

People have said to me, "Give treatments to change my husband, or my brother." I reply, "No, I will give **treatments to change you;** when you change, your husband and your brother will change."

One of my students was in the habit of lying. I told her it was a failure method and if she lied, she would be lied to. She replied, "I don't care, I can't possibly get along without lying."

One day she was speaking on the 'phone to a man with whom she was very much in love. She turned to me and said, "I don't trust him, I know he's lying to me." I replied, "Well, you lie yourself, so someone has to lie to you, and you will be sure it will be just the person you want the truth from." Sometime after that, I saw her, and she said, "I'm cured of lying."

I questioned: "What cured you?"

She replied: "I have been living with a woman who lied worse than I did!"

One is often cured of his faults by seeing them in others.

Life is a mirror, and we find only ourselves reflected in our associates.

Living in the past is a failure method and a violation of spiritual law.

Jesus Christ said, "Behold, now is the accepted time." "Now is the day of Salvation."

Lot's wife looked back and was turned into a pillar of salt.

The robbers of time are the past and the future. Man should bless the past, and forget it, if it keeps him in bondage, and bless the future, knowing it has in store for him endless joys, but live *fully in the now*.

For example: A woman came to me, complaining that she had no money with which to buy Christmas gifts. She said, "Last year was so different; I had plenty of money and gave lovely presents, and this year I have scarcely a cent." I replied, "You will never demonstrate money while you are pathetic and live in the past. Live fully in the **now**, and **get ready to give Christmas presents.** Dig your ditches, and the money will come." She exclaimed, "I know what to do! I will buy some tinsel twine, Christmas seals and wrapping paper." I replied, "Do that, and the **presents will come and stick themselves to the Christmas seals."**

This too, was showing financial fearlessness and faith in God, as the reasoning mind said, "Keep every cent you have, as you are not sure you will get any more." She bought the seals, paper and twine, and a few days before Christmas, received a gift of several hundred dollars. Buying the seals and twine had impressed the subconscious with expectancy, and opened the way for the manifestation of the money. She purchased all the presents in plenty of time.

Man must live suspended in the moment.

"Look well, therefore, to this Day! Such is the salutation of the Dawn."

He must be spiritually alert, ever awaiting his leads, taking advantage of every opportunity.

One day, I said continually (silently), "Infinite Spirit, don't let me miss a trick," and something very important was told to me that evening. It is most necessary to begin the day with right words.

Make an affirmation immediately upon waking.

For example: **"Thy will be done this day! Today is a day of completion, I give thanks for this perfect day, miracle shall follow miracle and wonders shall never cease."** Make this a habit, and one will see wonders and miracles come into his life.

One morning I picked up a book and read, "Look with wonder at that which is before you!" It seemed to be my message for the day, so I repeated again and again, "Look with wonder at that which is before you."

At about noon, a large sum of money, was given me, which I had been desiring for a certain purpose.

In a following chapter, I will give affirmations that I have found most effective. However, one should never use an affirmation unless it is absolutely satisfying and convincing to his own consciousness, and often an affirmation is changed to suit different people.

For example: The following has brought success to many:

"I have a wonderful work, in a wonderful way, I give wonderful service, for wonderful pay!"

I gave the first two lines to one of my students, and she added the last two.

It made a **most powerful statement,** as there should always be perfect payment for perfect service, and a rhyme sinks easily into the subconscious. She went about singing it aloud and soon did receive wonderful work in a wonderful way, and gave wonderful service for wonderful pay.

Another student, a business man, took it, and changed the word work to business.

He repeated, "I have a wonderful business, in a wonderful way, and I give wonderful service for wonderful pay." That afternoon he made a forty-one thousand dollar deal, though there had been no activity in his affairs for months. Every affirmation must be carefully worded and completely "cover the ground."

For example: I knew a woman, who was in great need, and made a demand for work. She received a great deal of work, but was never paid anything. She now knows to add, "wonderful service for wonderful pay."

It is man's divine right to have plenty! More than enough! "His barns should be full, and his cup should flow over!" This is God's idea for man, and when man breaks down the barriers of lack in his own consciousness, the Golden Age will be his, and every righteous desire of his heart fulfilled!

5
THE LAW OF KARMA AND THE LAW OF FORGIVENESS

Man receives only that which he gives. The Game of Life is a game of boomerangs. Man's thoughts, deeds and words, return to him sooner or later, with astounding accuracy. This is the law of Karma, which is Sanskrit for

"Comeback." "Whatsoever a man soweth, that shall he also reap."

For example: A friend told me this story of herself, illustrating the law. She said, "I make all my Karma on my aunt, whatever I say to her, someone says to me. I am often irritable at home, and one day, said to my aunt, who was talking to me during dinner. 'No more talk, I wish to eat in peace.'"

"The following day, I was lunching with a woman with whom I wished to make a great impression. I was talking animatedly, when she said: 'No more talk, I wish to eat in peace!'"

My friend is high in consciousness, so her Karma returns much more quickly than to one on the mental plane.

The more man knows, the more he is responsible for, and a person with a knowledge of Spiritual Law, which he does not practice, suffers greatly, in consequence. "The fear of the Lord (law) is the beginning of wisdom." If we read the word Lord, law, it will make many passages in the Bible much clearer.

"Vengeance is mine, I will repay saith the Lord" (law). It is the law which takes vengeance, not God. God sees man perfect, "created in his own image," (imagination) and given "power and dominion."

This is the perfect idea of man, registered in Divine Mind, awaiting man's recognition; for man can only be what he sees himself to be, and only attain what he sees himself attaining.

"Nothing ever happens without an on-looker" is an ancient saying.

Man sees first his failure or success, his joy or sorrow, before it swings into visibility from the scenes set in his own imagination. We have observed this in the mother picturing disease for her child, or a woman seeing success for her husband.

Jesus Christ said, "And ye shall know the truth and the truth shall make you free."

So, we see freedom (from all unhappy conditions) comes through knowledge - a knowledge of Spiritual Law. Obedience precedes authority, and the law obeys man when he obeys the law. The law of electricity must be obeyed before it becomes man's servant. When handled ignorantly, it becomes man's deadly foe. *So with the laws of Mind!*

For example: A woman with a strong personal will, wished she owned a house which belonged to an acquaintance, and she often made mental pictures of herself living in the house. In the course of time, the man died and she moved into the house. Several years afterwards, coming into the knowledge of Spiritual Law, she said to me: "Do you think I had anything to do with that man's death?" I replied: "Yes, your desire was so strong, everything made way for it, but you paid your Karmic debt. Your husband, whom you loved devotedly, died soon after, and the house was a white elephant on your hands for years."

The original owner, however, could not have been affected by her thoughts had he been positive in the truth, nor her husband, but they were both under Karmic law. The woman should have said (feeling the great desire for the house), "Infinite Intelligence, give me the right house, equally as charming as this, the house **which is mine by divine right**."

The divine selection would have given perfect satisfaction and brought good to all. The divine pattern is the only safe pattern to work by.

Desire is a tremendous force, and must be directed in the right channels, or chaos ensues.

In demonstrating, the most important step is the **first step, to "ask aright."**

Man should always demand only that which is his by **divine right.**

To go back to the illustration: Had the woman taken this attitude: "If this house, I desire, is mine, I cannot lose it, if it is not, give me its equivalent," the man might have decided to move out, harmoniously (had it been the divine selection for her) or another house would have been substituted. Anything forced into manifestation through personal will, is always "ill-got," and has "ever bad success."

Man is admonished, "My will be done not thine," and the curious thing is, man always gets just what he desires when he does relinquish personal will, thereby enabling Infinite Intelligence to work through him.

"Stand ye still and see the salvation of the Lord" (law).

For example: A woman came to me in great distress. Her daughter had determined to take a very hazardous trip, and the mother was filled with fear.

She said she had used every argument, had pointed out the dangers to be encountered, and forbidden her to go, but the daughter became more and more rebellious and determined. I said to the mother, "You are forcing your personal will upon your daughter, which you have no right to do, and your fear of the trip is only attracting it, for man attracts what he fears." I added, "Let go, and take your mental hands off; **put it in God's Hands, and use this statement:"** "I put this situation in the hands of Infinite Love and Wisdom; if this trip is the Divine plan, I bless it and no longer resist, but if it is not divinely planned, I give thanks that it is now dissolved and dissipated."

A day or two after that, her daughter said to her, "Mother, I have given up the trip," and the situation returned to its "native nothingness."

It is learning to "stand still," which seems so difficult for man. I have dealt more fully with this law in the chapter on nonresistance.

I will give another example of sowing and reaping, which came in the most curious way.

A woman came to me saying, she had received a counterfeit twenty-dollar bill, given to her at the bank. She was much disturbed, for, she said, "The people at the bank will never acknowledge their mistake."

I replied, "Let us analyze the situation and find out why you attracted it." She thought a few moments and exclaimed: "I know it, I sent a friend a lot of stage-money, just for a joke." So the law had sent her some stage-money, for it doesn't know anything about jokes.

I said, "Now we will call on the law of forgiveness, and neutralize the situation."

Christianity is founded upon the law of forgiveness - Christ has redeemed us from the curse of the Karmic law, and the Christ within each man is his Redeemer and Salvation from all inharmonious conditions.

So I said: "Infinite Spirit, we call on the law of forgiveness and give thanks that she is under grace and not under law, and cannot lose this twenty dollars which is hers by divine right."

"Now," I said, "Go back to the bank and tell them, fearlessly, that it was given you, there by mistake." She obeyed, and to her surprise, they apologized and gave her another bill, treating her most courteously.

So knowledge of the Law gives man power to "rub out his mistakes." Man cannot force the external to be what he is not.

If he desires riches, he must be rich first in consciousness. For example: A woman came to me asking treatment for prosperity. She did not take much interest in her household affairs, and her home was in great disorder.

I said to her, "If you wish to be rich, you much be orderly. All men with great wealth are orderly - and order is heaven's first law." I added, "You will never become rich with a burnt match in the pin-cushion." She had a good sense of humor and commenced immediately, putting her house in order. She rearranged furniture, straightened out bureau drawers, cleaned rugs, and soon made a big financial demonstration - a gift from a relative. The woman, herself, became made over, and keeps herself keyed-up financially, by being ever watchful of the **external and expecting prosperity, knowing God is her supply.**

Many people are in ignorance of the fact that gifts and things are investments, and that hoarding and saving invariably lead to loss.

"There is that scattereth and yet increaseth; and there is that withholdeth more than is meet, but it tendeth to poverty." For example: I knew a man who wanted to buy a fur-lined overcoat. He and his wife went to various shops, but there was none he wanted. He said they were all too cheap-looking. At last, he was shown one, the salesman said was valued at a thousand dollars, but which the manager would sell him for five-hundred dollars, as it was late in the season.

His financial possessions amounted to about seven hundred dollars. The reasoning mind would have said, "You can't afford to spend nearly all you have on a coat," but he was very intuitive and never reasoned.

He turned to his wife and said, "If I get this coat, I'll make a ton of money!" So his wife consented, weakly.

About a month later, he received a ten-thousand-dollar commission. The coat made him feel so rich, it linked him with success and prosperity; without the coat he would not have received the commission. It was an investment paying large dividends!

If man ignores these leadings to spend or to give, the same amount of money will go in an uninteresting or unhappy way.

For example: A woman told me, on Thanksgiving Day, she informed her family that they could not afford a Thanksgiving dinner. She had the money, but decided to save it.

A few days later, someone entered her room and took from the bureau drawer the exact amount the dinner would have cost.

The law always stands back of the man who spends fearlessly, with wisdom.

For example: One of my students was shopping with her little nephew. The child clamored for a toy, which she told him she could not afford to buy.

She realized suddenly that she was seeking lack, and not recognizing God as her supply!

So she bought the toy, and on her way home, picked **up, in the street, the exact amount of money she had paid for it.** Man's supply is inexhaustible and unfailing when fully trusted, but faith or trust must precede the demonstration. "According to your faith be it unto you." "Faith is the substance of things hoped for, the evidence of things not seen - " for faith holds the vision steady, and the adverse pictures are dissolved and dissipated, and "in due season we shall reap, if we faint not."

Jesus Christ brought the good news (the gospel) that there was a higher law than the law of Karma - and that that law transcends the law of Karma. It is the law of grace, or forgiveness. It is the law which *frees man from the law of cause and effect - the law of consequence. "Under grace, and not under law."*

We are told that on this plane, man reaps where he has not sown; the gifts of God are simply poured out upon him. "All that the Kingdom affords is his." This continued state of bliss awaits the man who has overcome the race (or world) thought.

In the world thought there is tribulation, but Jesus Christ said: "Be of good cheer; I have overcome the world." The world thought is that of sin, sickness and death. He saw their absolute unreality and said sickness and sorrow shall pass away and death itself, the last enemy, be overcome.

We know now, from a scientific standpoint, that death could be overcome by stamping the subconscious mind with the conviction of eternal youth and eternal life.

The subconscious, being simply power without direction, **_carries out orders without questioning._**

Working under the direction of the superconscious (the Christ or God within man) the "resurrection of the body" would be accomplished.

Man would no longer throw off his body in death, it would be transformed into the "body electric," sung by Walt Whitman, for Christianity is founded upon the forgiveness of sins and "an empty tomb."

6

CASTING THE BURDEN.
IMPRESSING THE SUBCONSCIOUS

When man knows his own powers and the workings of his mind, his great desire is to find an easy and quick way to impress the subconscious with good, for simply an intellectual knowledge of the Truth will not bring results. In my own case, I found the easiest way is in "casting the burden."

A metaphysician once explained it in this manner. He said, "The only thing which gives anything weight in nature, is the law of gravitation, and if a boulder could be taken high above the planet, there would be no weight in that boulder; and that is what Jesus Christ meant when he said: "My yoke is easy and my burden is light."

He had overcome the world vibration, and functioned in the fourth dimensional realm, where there is only perfection, completion, life and joy.

He said: "Come to me all ye that are labor and are heavy laden, and I will give you rest." "Take my yoke upon you, for my yoke is easy and my burden is light."

We are also told in the fifty-fifth Psalm, to "cast thy burden upon the Lord." Many passages in the Bible state that the **battle is God's** not man's and that man is always to *"stand still" and see the Salvation of the Lord.*

This indicates that the superconscious mind (or Christ within) is the department which fights man's battle and relieves him of burdens.

We see, therefore, that man violates law if he carries a burden, and a burden is an adverse thought or condition, and this thought or condition has its root in the subconscious.

It seems almost impossible to make any headway directing the subconscious from the conscious, or reasoning mind, as the reasoning mind (the intellect) is limited in its conceptions, and filled with doubts and fears.

How scientific it then is, to cast the burden upon the superconscious mind (or Christ within) where it is "made light," or dissolved into its native nothingness." For example: A woman in urgent need of money, "made light" upon the Christ within, the superconscious, with the statement, "I cast this burden of lack on the Christ (within) and I go free to have plenty!"

The belief in lack was her burden, and as she cast it upon the Superconscious with its belief of plenty, an avalanche of supply was the result.

We read, "The Christ in you the hope of glory." Another example: One of my students had been given a new piano, and there was no room in her studio for it until she had moved out the old one. She was in a state of perplexity. She wanted to keep the old piano, but knew of no place to send it. She became desperate, as the new piano was to be sent immediately; in fact, was on its way, with no place to put it. She said it came to her to repeat, "I cast this burden on the Christ within, and I go free."

A few moments later, her 'phone rang, and a woman friend asked if she might rent her old piano, and it was moved out, a few minutes before the new one arrived.

I knew a woman, whose burden was resentment. She said, "I cast this burden of resentment on the Christ within, and I go free, to be loving, harmonious and happy." The Almighty superconscious, flooded the subconscious with love, and her whole life was changed. For years, resentment had held her in a state of torment and imprisoned her soul (the subconscious mind).

The statement should be made over and over and over, sometimes for hours at a time, silently or audibly, with quietness but determination.

I have often compared it to winding-up a victrola. We must wind ourselves up with spoken words.

I have noticed, in "casting the burden," after a little while, one seems to see clearly. It is impossible to have clear vision, while in the throes of carnal mind. doubts and fear poison the mind and body and imagination runs riot, attracting disaster and disease.

In steadily repeating the affirmation, "I cast this burden on the Christ within, and go free," the vision clears, and with it a feeling of relief, and sooner or later comes **the manifestation of good, be it health, happiness or supply.**

One of my students once asked me to explain the "darkness before the dawn." I referred in a preceding chapter to the fact that often, before the big demonstration "everything seems to go wrong," and deep depression clouds the consciousness. It means that out of the subconscious are rising th doubts and fears of the ages. These old derelicts of the subconscious rise to the surface, to be put out.

It is then that man should clap his cymbals, like

Jehoshaphat, and give thanks that he is saved, even though he seems surrounded by the enemy (the situation of lack or disease). The student continued, "How long must one remain in the dark" and I replied, "until one **can see in the dark,** and **"casting the burden enables one to see in the dark."**

In order to impress the subconscious, active faith is always essential.

"Faith without works is dead." In these chapters I have endeavored to bring out this point.

Jesus Christ showed active faith when "He commanded the multitude to sit down on the ground," before he gave thanks for the loaves and fishes.

I will give another example showing how necessary this step is. In fact, active faith is the bridge, over which man passes to his Promised Land.

Through misunderstanding, a woman had been separated from her husband, whom she love deeply. He refused all offers of reconciliation and would not communicate with her in any way.

Coming into the knowledge of Spiritual law, she denied the appearance of separation. She made this statement: "There is no separation in Divine Mind, therefore, I cannot be separated from the love and companionship which are mine by divine right."

She showed active faith by arranging a place for him at the table every day; thereby impressing the subconscious with a picture of his return. Over a year passed, but she never wavered, and one day he walked in.

The subconscious is often impressed through music. Music has a fourth dimensional quality and releases the soul from imprisonment. It makes wonderful things seem ***possible, and easy of accomplishment!***

I have a friend who uses her victrola, daily, for this purpose. It puts her in perfect harmony and releases the imagination.

Another woman often dances while making her affirmations. The rhythm and harmony of music and motion carry her words forth with tremendous power.

The student must remember also, not to despise the "day of small things."

Invariably, before a demonstration, come "signs of land." Before Columbus reached America, he saw birds and twigs which showed him land was near. So it is with a demonstration; but often the student mistakes it for the demonstration itself, and is disappointed.

For example: A woman had "spoken the word" for a set of dishes. Not long afterwards a friend gave her a dish which was old and cracked.

She came to me and said, "Well, I asked for a set of dishes, and all I got was a cracked plate."

I replied, "The plate was only signs of land. It shows your dishes are coming - look upon it as a birds and seaweed," and not long afterwards the dishes came.

Continually "making-believe," impresses the subconscious. If one makes believe he is rich, and makes believe he is successful, in "due time he will reap."

Children are always "making believe," and "except ye be converted, and become as little children, ye shall not enter the Kingdom of Heaven."

For example: I know of a woman who was very poor, but no one could make her feel poor. She earned a small amount of money from rich friends, who constantly reminded her of her poverty, and to be careful and saving. Regardless of their admonitions, she would spend all her earnings on a hat, or make someone a gift, and be in a rapturous state of mind. Her thoughts were always centered on beautiful clothes and "rings and things," but without envying others.

She lived in the world of the wondrous, and only riches seemed real to her. Before long she married a rich man, and the rings and things became visible. I do not know whether the man was the "Divine Selection," but opulence had to manifest in her life, as she had imaged only opulence.

There is no peace or happiness for man, until he has erased all fear from the subconscious.

Fear is misdirected energy and must be redirected, or transmuted into Faith.

Jesus Christ said, "Why are ye fearful, O ye of little faith?" "All things are possible to him that believeth."

I am asked, so often by my students, "How can I get rid of fear?"

I reply, "By walking up to the thing you are afraid of."

"The lion takes its fierceness from your fear."

Walk up to the lion, and he will disappear; run away and he runs after you.

I have shown in previous chapters, how the lion of lack disappeared when the individual spent money fearlessly, showing faith that God was his supply and therefore, unfailing.

Many of my students have come out of the bondage of poverty, and are now bountifully supplied, through losing all fear of letting money go out. The subconscious is impressed with the truth that *God is the Giver and Gift*; therefore as one is one with the Giver, he is one with the Gift. A splendid statement is, "I now thank God the Giver for God the Gift."

Man has so long separated himself from his good and his supply, through thoughts of separation and lack, that sometimes, it takes dynamite to dislodge these false ideas from the subconscious, and the dynamite is a big situation.

We see in the foregoing illustration, how the individual was freed from his bondage by *showing fearlessness.*

Man should watch himself hourly to detect if his motive for action is fear or faith.

"Choose ye this day whom we shall serve," fear or faith.

Perhaps one's fear is of personality. Then do not avoid the people feared; be willing to meet them cheerfully, and they will either prove "golden links in the chain of one's good," or disappear harmoniously from one's pathway.

Perhaps one's fear is of disease or germs. Then one should be fearless and undisturbed in a germ-laden situation, and he would be immune.

One can only contract germs while vibrating at the same rate as the germ, and fear drags men down to the level of the germ. Of course, the disease laden germ is the product of carnal mind, as all thought must objectify. Germs do not exist in the superconscious or Divine Mind, therefore are the product of man's "vain imagination."

"In the twinkling of an eye," man's release will come when he realizes *there is no power in evil.*

The material world will fade away, and the fourth dimensional world, the "World of the Wondrous," will swing into manifestation.

"And I saw a new heaven, and a new earth - and there shall be no more death, neither sorrow nor crying, neither shall there be any more pain; for the former things are passed away."

7
LOVE

Every man on this planet is taking his initiation in love. "A new commandment I give unto you, that ye love one another." Ouspensky states, in "Tertium Organum," that "love is a cosmic phenomenon," and opens to man the fourth dimensional world, "The World of the Wondrous." Real love is selfless and free from fear. It pours itself out upon the object of its affection, without demanding any return. Its joy is in the joy of giving. Love is God in manifestation, and the strongest magnetic force in the universe. Pure, unselfish love **draws to itself its own**; it does not need to seek or demand. Scarcely anyone has the faintest conception of real love. Man is selfish, tyrannical or fearful in his affections, thereby losing the thing he loves. Jealousy is the worst enemy of love, for the imagination runs riot, seeing the loved one attracted to another, and invariably these fears objectify if they are not neutralized.

For example: A woman came to me in deep distress. The man she loved had left her for other women, and said he never intended to marry her. She was torn with jealousy and resentment and said she hoped he would suffer as he had made her suffer; and added, "How could he leave me when I loved him so much?"

I replied, "You are not loving that man, you are hating him," and added, "**You can never receive what you have never given. Give a perfect love and you will receive a perfect love.** Perfect yourself on this man. Give him a perfect, unselfish love, demanding nothing in return, do not criticize or condemn, and **bless him wherever his is.**" She replied, "No, I won't bless him unless I know where he is!" she said.

"Well," I said, "that is not real love."

"When you **send out real love,** real love will return to you, either from this man or his equivalent, for if this man is not the divine selection, you will not want him. As you are one with God, you are one with the love which belongs to you by divine right."

Several months passed, and matters remained about the same, but she was working conscientiously with herself. I said, "When you are no longer disturbed by his cruelty, he will cease to be cruel, as you are attracting it through your own emotions."

Then I told her of a brotherhood in India, who never said, "Good Morning" to each other. They used these words: **"I salute the Divinity in you."** They saluted the divinity in every man, and in the wild animals in the jungle, and they were never harmed, for they **saw only God in every** living thing. I said, "Salute the divinity in this man, and say, 'I see your divine self only. I see you as God see you, perfect, made in His image and likeness.'"

She found she was becoming more poised, and gradually losing her resentment. He was a Captain, and she always called him "The Cap."

One day, she said, suddenly, "***God bless the Cap wherever he is.***"

I replied: "Now that is real love, and when you have become a 'complete circle,' and are no longer disturbed by the situation, you will have his love, or attract its equivalent."

I was moving at this time, and did not have a telephone, so was out of touch with her for a few weeks, when one morning I received a letter saying, "We are married." At the earliest opportunity, I paid her a call. My first words were, "What happened?"

"Oh," she exclaimed, "a miracle! One day I woke up and all suffering had ceased. I saw him that evening and he asked me to marry him. We were married in about a week, and I have never seen a more devoted man."

There is an old saying: "***No man is your enemy, no man is your friend, every man is your teacher.***"

So one should become impersonal and learn what each man has to teach him, and soon he would learn his lessons and be free.

The woman's lover was teaching her selfless love, which every man, sooner or later, must learn.

Suffering is not necessary for man's development; it is the result of violation of spiritual law, but few people seem able to rouse themselves from their "soul sleep" without it. When people are happy, they usually become selfish, and automatically the law of Karma is set in action. Man often suffers loss through lack of appreciation.

I knew a woman who had a very nice husband, but she said often, "I don't care anything about being married, but that is nothing against my husband. I'm simply not interested in married life."

She had other interests, and scarcely remembered she had a husband. She only thought of him when she saw him. One day her husband told her he was in love with another woman, and left. She came to me in distress and resentment.

I replied, "It is exactly what you spoke the word for. You said you didn't care anything about being married, so the subconscious worked to get you unmarried."

She said, "Oh yes, I see. People get what they want, and then feel very much hurt."

She soon became in perfect harmony with the situation, and knew they were both much happier apart.

When a woman becomes indifferent or critical, and ceases to be an inspiration to her husband, he misses the stimulus of their early relationship and is restless and unhappy.

A man came to me dejected, miserable and poor. His wife was interested in the "Science of Numbers," and had had him read. It seems the report was not very favorable, for he said, "My wife says I'll never amount to anything because I am a two."

I replied, "I don't care what your number is, you are a perfect idea in divine mind, and we will demand the success and prosperity which are already planned for you by that Infinite Intelligence."

Within a few weeks, he had a very fine position, and a year or two later, he achieved a brilliant success as a writer. No man is a success in business unless he loves his work. The picture the artist paints for love (of his art) is his greatest work. The pot-boiler is always something to live down.

No man can attract money if he despises it. Many people are kept in poverty by saying: "Money means nothing to me, and I have a contempt for people who have it." This is the reason so many artists are poor. Their contempt for money separates them from it.

I remember hearing one artist say of another, "He's no good as an artist, he has money in the bank."

This attitude of mind, of course, separates man from his supply; he must be in harmony with a thing in order to attract it.

Money is God in manifestation, as freedom from want and limitation, but it must be always kept in circulation and put to right uses. Hoarding and saving react with grim vengeance.

This does not mean that man should not have houses and lots, stocks and bonds, for "the barns of the righteous man shall be full." It means man should not hoard even the principal, if an occasion arises, when money is necessary. In letting it go out fearlessly and cheerfully he opens the way for more to come in, for God is man's unfailing and inexhaustible supply.

This is the spiritual attitude towards money and the great Bank of the Universal never fails!

We see an example of hoarding in the film production of "Greed." The woman won five thousand dollars in a lottery, but would not spend it. She hoarded and saved, let her husband suffer and starve, and eventually she scrubbed floors for a living.

She loved the money itself and put it above everything, and one night she was murdered and the money taken from her. This is an example of where "love of money is the root of all evil." Money in itself, is good and beneficial, but used for destructive purposes, hoarded and saved, or considered more important than love, brings disease and disaster, and the loss of the money itself.

Follow the path of love, and all things are added, *for God is love, and God is supply*; follow the path of selfishness and greed, and the supply vanishes, or man is separated from it.

For example; I knew the case of a very rich woman, who hoarded her income. She rarely gave anything away, but bought and bought things for herself.

She was very fond of necklaces, and a friend once asked her how many she possessed. She replied, "Sixty-seven." She bought them and put them away, carefully wrapped in tissue paper. Had she used the necklaces it would have been quite legitimate, but she was violating "the law of use." Her closets were filled with clothes she never wore, and jewels which never saw the light.

The woman's arms were gradually becoming paralyzed from holding on to things, and eventually she was considered incapable of looking after her affairs and her wealth was handed over to others to manage. So man, in ignorance of the law, brings about his own destruction.

All disease, all unhappiness, come from the violation of the law of love. Man's boomerangs of hate, resentment and criticism, come back laden with sickness and sorrow. Love seems almost a lost art, but the man with the knowledge of spiritual law knows it must be regained, for without it, he has "become as sounding brass and tinkling cymbals." For example: I had a student who came to me, month after month, to clean her consciousness of resentment. After a while, she arrived at the point where she resented only one woman, but that one woman kept her busy. Little by little she became poised and harmonious, and one day, all resentment was wiped out.

She came in radiant, and exclaimed "You can't understand how I feel! The woman said something to me and instead of being furious I was loving and kind, and she apologized and was perfectly lovely to me.

No one can understand the marvelous lightness I feel within!"

Love and good-will are invaluable in business.

For example: A woman came to me, complaining of her employer. She said she was cold and critical and knew she did not want her in the position.

"Well," I replied, "Salute the Divinity in the woman and send her love."

She said "I can't; she's a marble woman."

I answered, "You remember the story of the sculptor who asked for a certain piece of marble. He was asked why he wanted it, and he replied, 'because there is an angel in the marble,' and out it he produced a wonderful work of art." She said, "Very well, I'll try it." A week later she came back and said, "I did what you told me to, and now the woman is very kind, and took me out in her car." People are sometimes filled with remorse for having done someone an unkindness, perhaps years ago.

If the wrong cannot be righted, its effect can be neutralized by doing some one a kindness *in the present.*

"This one thing I do, forgetting those things which are behind and reaching forth unto things where are before."

Sorrow, regret and remorse tear down the cells of the body, and poison the atmosphere of the individual.

A woman said to me in deep sorrow, "Treat me to be happy and joyous, for my sorrow makes me so irritable with members of my family that I keep making more Karma." I was asked to treat a woman who was mourning for her daughter. I denied all belief in loss and separation, and affirmed that God was the woman's joy, love and peace.

The woman gained her poise at once, but sent word by her son, not to treat any longer, because she was "so happy, it wasn't respectable."

So "mortal mind" loves to hang on to its griefs and regrets." I knew a woman who went about bragging of her troubles, so, of course, she always had something to brag about. The old idea was if a woman did not worry about her children, she was not a good mother.

Now, we know that mother-fear is responsible for many of the diseases and accidents which come into the lives of children.

For fear pictures vividly the disease or situation feared, and these pictures objectify, if not neutralized.

Happy is the mother who can say sincerely, that she puts her child in God's hands, and knows therefore, that he is divinely protected.

For example: A woman awoke suddenly, in the night, feeling her brother was in great danger. Instead of giving in to her fears, she commenced making statements of Truth, saying, "Man is a perfect idea in Divine Mind, and is always in his right place, therefore, my brother is in his right place, and is divinely protected."

The next day she found that her brother had been in close proximity to an explosion in a mine, but had miraculously escaped.

So man is his brother's keeper (in thought) and every man should know that the thing he loves dwells in "the secret place of the most high, and abides under the shadow of the Almighty."

"There shall no evil befall thee, neither shall any plague come nigh thy dwelling."

"Perfect love casteth out fear. He that feareth is not made perfect in love," and "Love is the fulfilling of the Law."

8
INTUITION OR GUIDANCE

There is nothing too great of accomplishment for the man who knows the power of his word, and who follows his intuitive leads. By the word he starts in action unseen forces and can rebuild his body or remold his affairs. It is, therefore, of the utmost importance, to choose the right words, and the student carefully selects the affirmation he wishes to catapult into the invisible.

He knows that God is his supply, that there is a supply for every demand, and that his spoken word releases this supply.

"Ask and ye shall receive."

Man must make the first move. "Draw nigh to God and He will draw nigh to you."

I have often been asked just how to make a demonstration. I reply: "Speak the word and then do not do anything until you get a definite lead." Demand the lead, saying, "Infinite spirit, reveal to me the way, let me know if there is anything for me to do."

The answer will come through intuition (or hunch); a chance remark from someone, or a passage in a book, etc., etc. The answers are sometimes quite startling in their exactness. For example: A woman desired a large sum of money. She spoke the words: "Infinite Spirit, open the way for my immediate supply, let all that is mine by divine right now reach me, in great avalanches of abundance." Then she added: "Give me a definite lead, let me know if there is anything for me to do."

The thought came quickly, "Give a certain friend" (who had helped her spiritually) "a hundred dollars." She told her friend, who said, "Wait and get another lead, before giving it." So she waited, and that day met a woman who said to her, "I gave someone a dollar today; it was just as much for me, as it would be for you to give someone a hundred." This was indeed an unmistakable lead, so she knew she was right in giving the hundred dollars. It was a gift which proved a great investment, for shortly after that, a large sum of money came to her in a remarkable way.

Giving opens the way for receiving. In order to create activity in finances, one should give. Tithing or giving one-tenth of one's income, is an old Jewish custom, and is sure to bring increase. Many of the richest men in this country have been tithers, and I have never known it to fail as an investment.

The tenth-part goes forth and returns blessed and multiplied. But the gift or tithe must be given with love and cheerfulness, for "God loveth a cheerful giver." Bills should be paid cheerfully, all money should be sent forth fearlessly and with a blessing.

This attitude of mind makes man master of money. It is his to obey, and his spoken word then opens vast reservoirs of wealth.

Man, himself, limits his supply by his limited vision. Sometimes the student has a great realization of wealth, but is afraid to act.

The vision and action must go hand in hand, as in the case of the man who bought the fur-lined overcoat.

A woman came to me asking me to "speak the word" for a position. So I demanded: "Infinite Spirit, open the way for this woman's right position." Never ask for just "a position"; ask for the right position, the place already planned in Divine Mind, as it is the only one that will give satisfaction.

I then gave thanks that she had already received, and that it would manifest quickly. Very soon, she had three positions offered her, two in New York and one in Palm Beach, and she did not know which to choose. I said, "Ask for a definite lead."

The time was almost up and was still undecided, when one day, she telephoned, "When I woke up this morning, I could smell Palm Beach." She had been there before and knew its balmy fragrance.

I replied: "Well, if you can smell Palm Beach from here, it is certainly your lead." She accepted the position, and it proved a great success. Often one's lead comes at an unexpected time.

One day, I was walking down the street, when I suddenly felt a strong urge to go to a certain bakery, a block or two away.

The reasoning mind resisted, arguing, "There is nothing there that you want."

However, I had learned not to reason, so I went to the bakery, looked at everything, and there was certainly nothing there that I wanted, but coming out I encountered a woman I had thought of often, and who was in great need of the help which I could give her.

So often, one goes for one thing and finds another.

Intuition is a spiritual faculty and does not explain, but simply **points the way**.

A person often receives a lead during a "treatment." The idea that comes may seem quite irrelevant, but some of God's leadings are "mysterious."

In the class, one day, I was treating that each individual would receive a definite lead. A woman came to me afterwards, and said: "While you were treating, I got the hunch to take my furniture out of storage and get an apartment." The woman had come to be treated for health. I told her I knew in getting a home of her own, her health would improve, and I added, "I believe your trouble, which is a congestion, has come from having things stored away. Congestion of things causes congestion in the body. You have violated the law of use, and your body is paying the penalty."

So I gave thanks that "**Divine order was established in her mind, body and affairs.**"

People little dream of how their affairs react on the body. There is a mental correspondence for every disease. A person might receive instantaneous healing through the realization of his body being a perfect idea in Divine Mind, and, therefore, whole and perfect, but if he continues his destructive thinking, hoarding, hating, fearing, condemning, the disease will return.

Jesus Christ knew that all sickness came from sin, but admonished the leper after the healing, to go and sin no more, lest a worse thing come upon him.

So man's soul (or subconscious mind) must be washed whiter than snow, for permanent healing; and the metaphysician is always delving deep for the "correspondence."

Jesus Christ said, "Condemn not lest ye also be condemned."

"Judge not, lest ye be judged."

Many people have attracted disease and unhappiness through condemnation of others.

What man condemns in others, he attracts to himself.

For example: A friend came to me in anger and distress, because her husband had deserted her for another woman. She condemned the other woman, and said continually, "She knew he was a married man, and had no right to accept his attentions."

I replied: "Stop condemning the woman, bless her, and be through with the situation, otherwise, you are attracting the same thing to yourself."

She was deaf to my words, and a year or two later, became deeply interested in a married man, herself.

Man picks up a live-wire whenever he criticizes or condemns, and may expect a shock.

Indecision is a stumbling-block in many a pathway. In order to overcome it, make the statement repeatedly, "*I am always under direct inspiration; I make right decisions, quickly.*"

These words impress the subconscious, and soon one finds himself awake and alert, making his right moves without hesitation. I have found it destructive to look to the psychic plane for guidance, as it is the plane of many minds and not the "The One Mind."

As man opens his mind to subjectivity, he becomes a target for destructive forces. The psychic plane is the result of man's mortal thought, and is on the "plane of opposites." He may receive either good or bad messages.

The science of numbers and the reading of horoscopes, keep man down on the mental (or mortal) plane, for they deal only with the Karmic path.

I know of a man who should have been dead, years ago, according to his horoscope, but he is alive and a leader of one of the biggest movements in this country for the uplift of humanity.

It takes a very strong mind to neutralize a prophecy of evil. The student should declare, "Every false prophecy shall come to naught; every plan my Father in heaven has not planned, shall be dissolved and dissipated, the divine idea now comes to pass."

However, if any good message has ever been given one, of coming happiness, or wealth, harbor and expect it, and it will manifest sooner or later, through the law of expectancy.

Man's will should be used to back the universal will. "I will that the will of God be done."

It is God's will to give every man, every righteous desire of his heart, and man's will should be used to hold the perfect vision, without wavering.

The prodigal son said: "I will arise and go to my Father." It is indeed, often an effort of the will to leave the husks and swine of mortal thinking. It is so much easier, for the average person, to have fear than faith; *so faith is an effort of the will*.

As man becomes spiritually awakened he recognizes that any external inharmony is the correspondence of mental inharmony. If he stumbles or falls, he may know he is stumbling or falling in consciousness.

One day, a student was walking along the street condemning someone in her thoughts. She was saying mentally, "That woman is the most disagreeable woman on earth," when suddenly three boy scouts rushed around the corner and almost knocked her over. She did not condemn the boy scouts, but immediately called on the law of forgiveness, and "saluted the divinity" in the woman. Wisdom's way are ways of pleasantness and all her paths are peace.

When one has made his demands upon the Universal, he must be ready for surprises. Everything may seem to be going wrong, when in reality, it is going right.

For example: A woman was told that there was no loss in divine mind, therefore, she could not lose anything which belonged to her; anything lost, would be returned, or she would receive its equivalent.

Several years previously, she had lost two thousand dollars. She had loaned the money to a relative during her lifetime, but the relative had died, leaving no mention of it in her will. The woman was resentful and angry, and as she had no written statement of the transaction, she never received the money, so she determined to deny the loss, and collect the two thousand dollars from the Bank of the Universal. She had to begin by forgiving the woman, as resentment and unforgiveness close the doors of this wonderful bank.

She made this statement, "I deny loss, there is no loss in Divine Mind, therefore, I cannot lose the two thousand dollars, which belong to me by divine right. "*As one door shuts another door opens*."

She was living in an apartment house which was for sale; and in the lease was a clause, stating that if the house was sold, the tenants would be required to move out within ninety days.

Suddenly, the landlord broke the leases and raised the rent. Again, injustice was on her pathway, but this time she was undisturbed. She blessed the landlord, and said, "As the rent has been raised, it means that I'll be that much richer, for God is my supply."

New leases were made out for the advanced rent, but by some divine mistake, the ninety days clause had been forgotten. Soon after, the landlord had an opportunity to sell the house. On account of the mistake in the new leases, the tenants held possession for another year.

The agent offered each tenant two hundred dollars if he would vacate. Several families moved; three remained, including the woman. A month or two passed, and the agent again appeared. This time he said to the woman, "Will you break your lease for the sum of fifteen hundred dollars?" It flashed upon her, "Here comes the two thousand dollars." She remembered having said to friends in the house, "We will all act together if anything more is said about leaving." So her lead was to consult her friends.

These friends said," Well, if they have offered you fifteen hundred they will certainly give two thousand." So she received a check for two thousand dollars for giving up the apartment. It was certainly a remarkable working of the law, and the apparent injustice was merely opening the way for her demonstration.

It proved that there is no loss, and when man takes his spiritual stand, he collects all that is his from this great Reservoir of Good.

"I will restore to you the years the locusts have eaten."

These adverse thoughts, alone, rob man; for "No man gives to himself but himself, and no man takes away from himself, but himself."

Man is here to prove God and "to bear witness to the truth," and he can only prove God by bringing plenty out of lack, and justice out of justice.

"Prove me now herewith, saith the Lord of hosts, if I will not open you the windows of heaven, and pour out a blessing, that there shall not be room enough to receive it."

9
PERFECT SELF EXPRESSION OR THE DIVINE DESIGN

There is for each man, perfect self-expression. There is a place which he is to fill and no one else can fill, something which he is to do, which no one else can do; it is his destiny!

This achievement is held, a perfect idea in Divine Mind, awaiting man's recognition. As the imaging faculty is the creative faculty, it is necessary for man to see the idea, before it can manifest.

So man's highest demand is for the *Divine Design of his life.*

He may not have the faintest conception of what it is, for there is, possibly, some marvelous talent, hidden deep within him.

His demand should be: *"Infinite Spirit, open the way for the Divine Design of my life to manifest; let the genius within me now be released; let me see clearly the perfect plan."*

The perfect plan includes health, wealth, love and perfect self-expression. This is the *square of life*, which brings perfect happiness. When one has made this demand, he may find great changes taking place in his life, for nearly every man has wandered far from the Divine Design.

I know, in one woman's case, it was as though a cyclone had struck her affairs, but readjustments came quickly, and new and wonderful conditions took the place of old ones. Perfect self-expression will never be labor; but of such absorbing interest that it will seem almost like play. The student knows, also, as man comes into the world financed by God, the *supply* needed for his perfect self-expression will be at hand.

Many a genius has struggled for years with the problem of supply, when his spoken word, and faith, would have released quickly, the necessary funds.

For example: After the class, one day, a man came to me and handed me a cent.

He said: "I have just seven cents in the world, and I'm going to give you one; for I have faith in the power of your spoken word. I want you to speak the word for my perfect self-expression and prosperity."

I "spoke the word," and did not see him again until a year later. He came in one day, successful and happy, with a roll of yellow bills in his pocket. He said, "Immediately after you spoke the word, I had a position offered me in a distant city, and am now demonstrating health, happiness and supply."

A woman's perfect self-expression may be in becoming a perfect wife, a perfect mother, a perfect home-maker and not necessarily in having a public career.

Demand definite leads, and the way will be made easy and successful.

One should not visualize or force a mental picture. When he demands the Divine Design to come into his conscious mind, he will receive flashes of inspiration, and begin to see himself making some great accomplishment. This is the picture, or idea, he must hold without wavering. The thing man seeks is seeking him - *the telephone was seeking Bell!*

Parents should never force careers and professions upon their children. With a knowledge of spiritual Truth, the Divine Plan could be spoken for, early in childhood, or prenatally.

A prenatal treatment should be: "Let the God in this child have perfect expression; let the Divine Design of his mind, body and affairs be made manifest throughout his life, throughout eternity."

God's will be done, not man's; God's pattern, not man's pattern, is the command we find running through all the scriptures, and the Bible is a book dealing with the science of the mind. It is a book telling man how to release his soul (or subconscious mind) from bondage.

The battles described are pictures of man waging war against mortal thoughts. "A man's foes shall be they of his own household." Every man is Jehoshaphat, and every man is David, who slays Goliath (mortal thinking) with the little white stone (faith).

So man must be careful that his is not the "wicked and slothful servant" who buried his talent. There is a terrible penalty to be paid for not using one's ability.

Often fear stands between man and his perfect self-expression. Stage-fright has hampered many a genius. This may be overcome by the spoken word or treatment. The individual then loses all self-consciousness, and feels simply that he is a channel for Infinite Intelligence to express Itself through.

He is under direct inspiration, fearless, and confident; for he feels that it is the "Father within" him who does the work.

A young boy came often to my class with his mother. He asked me to "speak the word" for his coming examinations at school.

I told him to make the statement: "I am one with Infinite Intelligence. I know everything I should know on this subject." He had an excellent knowledge of history, but was not sure of his arithmetic. I saw him afterwards, and he said: "I spoke the word for my arithmetic, and passed with the highest honors; but thought I could depend on myself for history, and got a very poor mark." Man often receives a set-back when he is "too sure of himself," which means he is trusting to his personality and not the "Father within."

Another one of my students gave me an example of this. She took an extended trip abroad one summer, visiting many countries, where she was ignorant of the languages.

She was calling for guidance and protection every minute, and her affairs went smoothly and miraculously. Her luggage was never delayed nor lost!

Accommodations were always ready for her at the best hotels; and she had perfect service wherever she went. She returned to New York. Knowing the language, she felt God was longer necessary, so looked after her affairs in an ordinary manner. Everything went wrong, her trunks delayed, amid inharmony and confusion. The student must form the habit of "practicing the Presence of God" every minute. "In all thy ways acknowledge him;" nothing is too small or too great.

Sometimes an insignificant incident may be the turning point in a man's life.

Robert Fulton, watching some boiling water, simmering in a tea kettle, saw a steamboat!

I have seen a student, often, keep back his demonstration, through resistance, or pointing the way.

He pins his faith to one channel only, and dictates just the way he desires the manifestation to come, which brings things to a standstill.

"My way, not your way!" is the command of Infinite Intelligence. Like all Power, be it steam or electricity, it must have a nonresistant engine or instrument to work through, and man is that engine or instrument.

Over and over again, man is told to "stand still". "Oh Judah, fear not; but to-morrow go out against them, for the lord will be with you. You shall not need to fight this battle; set yourselves, stand ye still, and see the salvation of the Lord with you."

We see this in the incidents of the two thousand dollars coming to the woman through the landlord when she became nonresistant and undisturbed, and the woman who won the man's love "after all suffering had ceased." The student's goal is Poise! Poise is Power, for it gives God-Power a chance to rush through man, to "will and to do Its good pleasure."

Poised, he thinks clearly, and makes "right decisions quickly." "He never misses a trick."

Anger blurs the visions, poisons the blood, is the root of many diseases, and causes wrong decision leading to failure.

It has been named one of the worst "sins," as its reaction is so harmful. The student learns that in metaphysics sin has a much broader meaning than in the old teaching. "Whatsoever is not of faith is sin."

He finds that fear and worry are deadly sins. The are inverted faith, and through distorted mental pictures, bring to pass the thing he fears. His work is to drive out these enemies (from the subconscious mind). "When Man is fearless he is finished!" Maeterlinck says, that "Man is God afraid."

So as we read in the previous chapters; man can only vanquish fear by walking up to the thing he is afraid of. When Jehoshaphat and his army prepared to meet the enemy, singing "Praise the Lord, for his mercy endureth forever," they found their enemies had destroyed each other, and there was nothing to fight.

For example: A woman asked a friend to deliver a message to another friend. The woman feared to give the message, as the reasoning mind said, "Don't get mixed-up in this affair, don't give that message."

She was troubled in spirit, for she had given her promise. At last, she determined to "walk up to the lion," and call on the law of divine protection. She met the friend to whom she was to deliver the message. She opened her mouth to speak it, when her friend said, "So and So has left town," This made it unnecessary to give the message, as the situation depended upon the person being in town. As she was willing to do it, she was not obliged to; as she did not fear, the situation vanished.

The student often delays his demonstration through a belief in incompletion. He should make this statement:

"In Divine Mind there is only completion, therefore, my demonstration is completed. My perfect work, my perfect home, my perfect health." Whatever he demands are perfect ideas registered in Divine Mind, and must manifest, "under grace in a perfect way." He gives thanks he has already received on the invisible, and makes active preparation for receiving on the visible.

One of my students was in need of a financial demonstration. She came to me and asked why it was not completed.

I replied: "Perhaps, you are in the habit of leaving things unfinished, and the subconscious has gotten into the habit of not completing (as the without, so the within)." "I'll go home and finish something I commenced weeks ago, and I know it will be symbolic of my demonstration." She sewed assiduously, and the article was soon completed. Shortly after, the money came in a most curious manner.

Her husband was paid his salary twice that month. He told the people of their mistake, and they sent word to keep it.

When man ask, *believing, he must receive, for God creates His own channels!*

I have been sometimes asked, "Suppose one has several talents, how is he to know which one to choose?" Demand to be shown definitely, Say: "Infinite Spirit, give me a definite lead, reveal to me my perfect self-expression, show me which talent I am to make use of now."

I have known people to suddenly enter a new line of work, and be fully equipped, with little or no training. So make the statement: *"I am fully equipped for the Divine Plan of my life,"* and be fearless in grasping opportunities.

Some people are cheerful givers, but bad receivers. They refuse gifts through pride, or some negative reason, thereby blocking their channels, and invariably find themselves eventually with little or nothing. For example: A woman who had given away a great deal of money, had a gift offered her of several thousand dollars. She refused to take it, saying she did not need it. Shortly after that, her finances were "tied up", and she found herself in debt for that amount. Man should receive gracefully the bread returning to him upon the water - freely ye have given, freely ye shall receive.

There is always the perfect balance of giving and receiving, and though man should give without thinking of returns, he violates law if he does not accept the returns which come to him; for all gifts are from God, man being merely the channel.

A thought of lack should never be held over the giver.

For example: When the man gave the one cent, I did not say; "Poor man, he cannot afford to give me that." I saw him rich and prosperous, with his supply pouring in. It was this thought which brought it. If one has been a bad receiver, he must become a good one, and take even a postage stamp if it is given him, and open up his channels for receiving.

The Lord loveth a cheerful receiver, as well as a cheerful giver.

I have often been asked why one man is born rich and healthy, and another poor and sick.

Where there is an effect there is always a cause; there is no such thing as chance.

This question is answered through the law of reincarnation. Man goes through many births and deaths, until he knows the truth which sets him free.

He is drawn back to the earth plane through unsatisfied desire, to pay his Karmic debts, or to "fulfill his destiny." The man born rich and healthy has had pictures in his subconscious mind, in his past life, of health and riches; and the poor and sick man, of disease and poverty. Man manifests, on any plane, the sum total of his subconscious beliefs.

However, birth and death are man-made laws, for the "wages of sin is death"; the Adamic fall in consciousness through the belief in **two powers.** The real man, spiritual man, is birthless and deathless! He never was born and has never died - "As he was in the beginning, he is now, and ever shall be!"

So through the truth, man is set free from the law of Karma, sin and death, and manifests the man made in "His image and likeness." Man's freedom comes through fulfilling his destiny, bringing into manifestation the Divine Design of his life.

His lord will say unto him: "Well done thou good and faithful servant, thou has been faithful over a few things, I will make thee ruler over many things (death itself); enter thou into in the joy of thy Lord (eternal life)."

10
DENIALS AND AFFIRMATIONS

Thou shalt decree a thing, and it shall be established unto thee."

All the good that is to be made manifest in man's life is already an accomplished fact in divine mind, and is released through man's recognition, or spoken word, so he must be careful to decree that only the Divine Idea be made manifest, for often, he decrees, through his "idle words," failure or misfortune.

It is, therefore, of the utmost importance, to word one's demands correctly, as stated in a previous chapter.

If one desires a home, friend, position or any other good thing, make the demand for the "divine selection."

For example: "Infinite Spirit, open the way for my right home, my right friend, my right position. I give thanks *it now manifests under grace in a perfect way.*" The latter part of the statement is most important. For example: I knew a woman who demanded a thousand dollars. Her daughter was injured and they received a thousand dollars indemnity, so it did not come in a "perfect way."

The demand should have been worded in this way: "Infinite Spirit, I give thanks that the one thousand dollars, which is mine by divine right, is now released, and reaches me under grace in a perfect way."

As one grows in a financial consciousness, he should demand that the enormous sums of money, which are his by divine right, reach him under grace, in perfect ways.

It is impossible for man to release more than he thinks is possible, for one is bound by the limited expectancies of the subconscious. He must enlarge his expectancies in order to receive in a larger way.

Man so often limits himself in his demands. For example: A student made the demand for six hundred dollars, by a certain date. He did receive it, but heard afterwards, that he came very near receiving a thousand dollars, but he was given just six hundred, as the result of his spoken word.

"They limited the Holy One of Israel." Wealth is a matter of consciousness. The French have a legend giving an example of this. A poor man was walking along a road when he met a traveler, who stopped him and said: "My good friend, I see you are poor. Take this gold nugget, sell it, and you will be rich all your days."

The man was overjoyed at his good fortune, and took the nugget home. He immediately found work and became so prosperous that he did not sell the nugget. Years passed, and he became a very rich man. One day he met a poor man on the road. He stopped him and said: "My good friend, I will give you this gold nugget, which, if you sell, will make you rich for life." The mendicant took the nugget, had it valued, and found it was only brass. So we see, the first man became rich through feeling rich, thinking the nugget was gold.

Every man has within himself a gold nugget; *it is his consciousness of gold, of opulence, which brings riches into his life.* In making his demands, man begins at his *journey's end*, that is he declares *he has already received.* *"Before"* ye call I shall answer."

Continually affirming establishes the belief in the subconscious.

It would not be necessary to make an affirmation more than once if one had perfect faith! One should not plead or supplicate, but give thanks repeatedly, that he has received.

"The desert shall rejoice and blossom as the rose." This rejoicing which is yet in the desert (state of consciousness) opens the way for release. The Lord's Prayer is in the form of command and demand, "Give us this day our daily bread, and forgive us our debts as we forgive our debtors," and ends in praise, "For thine is the Kingdom and the Power and the Glory, forever. Amen." "Concerning the works of my hands, command ye me." So prayer is command and demand, praise and thanksgiving. The student's work is in making himself believe that "with God all things are possible."

This is easy enough to state in the abstract, but a little more difficult when confronted with a problem. For example: It was necessary for a woman to demonstrate a large sum of money within a stated time. She knew she must *do something* to get a realization (for realization is manifestation), and she demanded a "lead."

She was walking through a department store, when she saw a very beautiful pink enamel papercutter. She felt the "pull" towards it. The thought came. "I haven't a paper cutter good enough to open letters containing large cheques." So she bought the papercutter, which the reasoning mind would have called an extravagance. When she held it in her hand, she had a flash of a picture of herself opening an envelope containing a large cheque, and in a few weeks, she received the money. The pink papercutter was her bridge of active faith.

Many stories are told of the power of the subconscious when directed in faith.

For example: A man was spending the night in a farmhouse. The windows of the room had been nailed down, and in the middle of the night he felt suffocated and made his way in the dark to the window. He could not open it, so he smashed the pane with his fist, drew in draughts of fine fresh air, and had a wonderful night's sleep. The next morning, he found he had smashed the glass of a bookcase and the window had remained closed during the whole night. He had *supplied himself with oxygen, simply by his thought of oxygen.*

When a student starts out to demonstrate, he should never turn back. "Let not that man who wavers think that he shall receive anything of the Lord."

A colored student once made this wonderful statement, "When I asks the Father for anything, I puts my foot down, and I says: Father, I'll take nothing less than I've asked for, but more!" So man should never compromise: "Having done all - Stand." This is sometimes the most difficult time of demonstrating. The temptation comes to give up, to turn back, to compromise.

"He also serves who only stands and waits."

Demonstrations often come at the eleventh hour because man then lets go, that is, stops reasoning, and Infinite Intelligence has a chance to work.

"Man's dreary desires are answered drearily, and his impatient desires, long delayed or violently fulfilled.

For example: A woman asked me why it was she was constantly losing or breaking her glasses.

We found she often said to herself and others with vexation, "I wish I could get rid of my glasses." So her impatient desire was violently fulfilled. What she should have demanded was perfect eye-sight, but what she registered in the subconscious was simply the impatient desire to be rid of her glasses; so they were continually being broken or lost.

Two attitudes of mind cause loss: depreciation, as in the case of the woman who did not appreciate her husband, *or fear of loss*, which makes a picture of loss in the subconscious.

When a student is able to let go of his problem (cast his burden) he will have instantaneous manifestation.

For example: A woman was out during a very stormy day and her umbrella was blown inside-out. She was about to make a call on some people whom she had never met and she did not wish to make her first appearance with a dilapidated umbrella. She could not throw it away, as it did not belong to her. So in desperation, she exclaimed: "Oh God, you take charge of this umbrella, I don't know what to do."

A moment later, a voice behind her said: "Lady, do you want your umbrella mended? There stood an umbrella mender.

She replied, "Indeed, I do."

The man mended the umbrella, while she went into the house to pay her call, and when she returned, she had a good umbrella. So there is always an umbrella mender at hand, on man's pathway, when one puts the umbrella (or situation) in God's Hands.

One should always follow a denial with an affirmation.

For example: I was called on the 'phone late one night to treat a man whom I had never seen. He was apparently very ill. I made the statement: "I deny this appearance of disease. It is unreal, therefore cannot register in his consciousness; this man is a perfect idea in Divine Mind, pure substance expressing perfection."

There is no time or space, in Divine Mind, therefore the word reaches instantly its destination and does not "return void." I have treated patients in Europe and have found that the result was instantaneous.

I am asked so often the difference between visualizing and visioning. Visualizing is a mental process governed by the reasoning or conscious mind; visioning is a spiritual process, governed by intuition, or the superconscious mind. The student should train his mind to receive these flashes of inspiration, and work out the "divine pictures," through definite leads. When a man can say, "I desire only that which God desires for me," his new set of blueprints is given him by the Master Architect, the God within. God's plan for each man transcends the limitation of the reasoning mind, and is always the square of life, containing health, wealth, love and perfect self-expression. Many a man is building for himself in imagination a bungalow when he should be building a palace.

If a student tries to force a demonstration (through the reasoning mind) he brings it to a standstill. "I will hasten it," saith the Lord. He should act only through intuition, or definite leads. "Rest in the Lord and wait patiently. Trust also in him, and he will bring it to pass."

I have seen the law work in the most astonishing manner. For example: A student stated that it was necessary for her to have a hundred dollars for the following day. It was a debt of vital importance which had to be met. I "spoke the word," declaring Spirit was "never too late" and that the supply was at hand.

That evening she phoned me of the miracle. She said that the thought came to her to go to her safe-deposit box at the bank to examine some papers. She looked over the papers, and at the bottom of the box, was a new one hundred dollar bill. She was astounded, and said she knew she had never put it there, for she had gone through the papers many times. It may have been a materialization, as Jesus Christ materialized the loaves and fishes. Man will reach the stage where his "word is made flesh," or materialized, instantly. "The fields, ripe with the harvest," will manifest immediately, as in all of the miracles of Jesus Christ.

There is a tremendous power alone in the name Jesus Christ. It stands for **Truth Made Manifest.** He said, "Whatsoever ye ask the Father, in my name, he will give it to you."

The power of this name raises the student into the fourth dimension, where he is freed from all astral and psychic influences, and he becomes "unconditioned and absolute, as God Himself is unconditioned and absolute." I have seen many healings accomplished by using the words, "In the name of Jesus Christ."

Christ was both person and principle; and the Christ within each man is his Redeemer and Salvation.

The Christ within, is his own fourth dimensional self, the man made in God's image and likeness. This is the self which has never failed, never known sickness or sorrow, was never born and has never died. It is the "resurrection and the life" of each man! "No man cometh to the Father save by the Son," means, that God, the Universal, working on the place of the particular, becomes the Christ in man; and the Holy Ghost, means God-in-action. So daily, man is manifesting the Trinity of Father, Son and Holy Ghost.

Man should make an art of thinking. The Master Thinker is an artist and is careful to paint only the divine designs upon the canvas of his mind; and he paints these pictures with masterly strokes of power and decision, having perfect faith that there is no power to mar their perfection and that they shall manifest in his life the ideal made real.

All power is given man (through right thinking) to bring *his heaven* upon *his earth,* and this is the *goal of the "Game of Life."*

The simple rules are fearless faith, nonresistance and love! May each reader be now freed from that thing which has held him in bondage through the ages, standing between him and his own, and "know the Truth which makes him free" - free to fulfill his destiny, to bring into manifestation the *"Divine Design of his life,* Health, Wealth, Love and Perfect Self-Expression." "Be ye transformed by the renewing of your mind."

Denials and Affirmations

For Prosperity

God is my unfailing supply, and large sums of money come to me quickly, under grace, in perfect ways.

For Right Conditions

Every plan my Father in heaven has not planned, shall be dissolved and dissipated, and the Divine Idea now comes to pass.

For Right Conditions

Only that which is true of God is true of me, for I and the Father are ONE.

For Faith

As I am one with God, I am one with my good, for God is both the *Giver* and the *Gift.* I cannot separate the Giver from the gift.

For Right Conditions

Divine Love now dissolves and dissipates every wrong condition in my mind, body and affairs. Divine Love is the most powerful chemical in the universe, and *dissolves everything* which is not of itself!

For Health

Divine Love floods my consciousness with health, and every cell in my body is filled with light.

For the Eyesight

My eyes are God's eyes, I see with the eyes of spirit. I see clearly the open way; there are no obstacles on my pathway. I see clearly the perfect plan.

For Guidance

I am divinely sensitive to my intuitive leads, and give instant obedience to Thy will.

For the Hearing

My ears are God's ears, I hear with the ears of spirit. I am nonresistant and am willing to be led. I hear glad tidings of great joy.

For Right Work

I have a perfect work
In a perfect way;
I give a perfect
service For perfect pay.

For Freedom from all Bondage

I cast this burden on the Christ within, and I go free!

THE END

Your Invisible Power,

Genevieve Behrend

THE HISTORY, INFLUENCES AND PRINCIPLES OF THE NEW THOUGHT MOVEMENT AND THE IMPORTANCE TO THE WORKS OF GENEVIEVE BEHREND

An introductory article, compiled by author Mauricio Chaves-Mesén

THE ORIGINS

The stem of New Thought appeared in the United States in the first part of the nineteenth century.

About 1800-25, there was in New England a revival of transcendental thought, traced directly to the interest in Arminianism and Arianism -evinced a full century before by New England thinkers. This interest spread out in two directions: the Unitarianism; and the Transcendental Movement of Emerson and his associates (based on a revived interest in Neo-Platonism).

New England thought began to escape from the influence of Locke and Bentham, which had dominated the philosophical thought; and to manifest new interest in the ideas of the newer schools of English and German thought. A similar revolution manifested in literature, and a keen interest began in the writings of Coleridge, Wordsworth, Herder, Goethe, and others who held certain ideas fitting well into the new conceptions.

These awakened New Englanders were attracted by Coleridge's idea of a higher reason (or *transcendental intuition),* a manifestation of the indwelling spirit. By its means one *"might experience an immediate perception of things above the plane of the ordinary senses and reason".* Coleridge also taught that there was a great Universal Spirit, reflected in the spirits of all men.

Wordsworth presented an attractive form of higher pantheism—a nature in which was immanent the One Spirit of the Universe; a universe animated by a Universal Mind, proceeding under Universal Law and Order.

SO, WHEN WAS NEW THOUGHT BORN?

The term "new thought" was used in that early day, not, however, as indicating a cult or particular school of thought, but rather as a term describing the newly awakened tendency, and in contrast to the "old thought" of Calvinism and the old schools of philosophy.

The early Unitarians also used the term "new thought" in the same way, as applied to their teachings.

This "new thought" began to take shape about 1830, when the various elements converged in what was afterward the *Transcendental Movement*.

Emerson's work had attracted much attention, and his writings served as a nucleus around which sympathetic thinkers grouped themselves. Frank

Channing, George Ripley, Ralph Waldo Emerson, Margaret Fuller, Brownson and Hedge, all well known in connection with the "new thought" of that day, met and considered the advisability of forming a general society. For a number of years their work created great interest, and a loosely organized following gathered around them.

The Brook Farm Community, founded by Ripley in 1841, played an important part in the work, attracting, as it did, such men and women as Hawthorne, Alcott, Curtis, Channing, and Margaret Fuller.

In 1840, "The Dial" journal was founded as official organ of the Transcendental Movement, and served to fasten the attention of the nation upon it and its principles. Margaret Fuller was the first editor, and Channing, Alcott, Theodore Parker, Ripley, Thoreau, and Emerson (who later became editor), among the contributors.

This time may be considered as the real date of the birth of the modern New Thought movement.

THE INFLUENCE OF EMERSON AND TRASCENDENTALISM

Transcendentalism is defined as: "The philosophical conception that there can be knowledge of transcendental elements, or matters wholly beyond the ordinary experience of the human mind." But the Transcendentalists went much further than this.

Margaret Fuller, in her memoirs, says: "Transcendentalism was an assertion of the inalienable integrity of man; of the immanence of Divinity in instinct ... On the somewhat stunted stock of Unitarianism, whose characteristic dogma was trust in human reason, as correlative to Supreme Wisdom, had been grafted German Idealism, as taught by masters of most various schools—by Kant and Jacobi, Fichte and Novalis, Schelling and Hegel, Schleirmacher and de Wette, by Madame de Stael, Cousin, Coleridge, and Carlyle; and the result was a vague yet exalting, conception of the god-like nature of the human spirit.

Transcendentalism, as viewed by its disciples, was a pilgrimage from the idolatrous world of creeds and rituals to the Temple of the Living God in the soul."

The essence of the Transcendental movement may be found in the essays of Emerson, particularly in his essay on the "OverSoul," in which is sounded the dominant note of the later New Thought. Emerson was essentially an idealist and a mystic. As Cooke says: "Emerson belongs in a succession of Idealists. That company he loves wherever its members are found, whether among Buddhists or Christian mystics, whether Transcendentalist or Sufi, whether Saadi, Boehme, Fichte, or Carlyle. These are the writers he studies, these the men he quotes, these the thinkers who come nearest his own thought. He is in the succession of minds who have followed in the wake of Plato, who is regarded by him as the world's greatest thinker. More directly still, Emerson is in that succession of thinkers represented by Plotinus, Eckhardt, and Schelling, who have interpreted Idealism in the form of Mysticism."

The broadness and catholicity of Emerson's thought descended in a direct line to the New Thought movement, which drew upon all sources for its truth, taking its own wherever it finds it, "whether on Christian or on heathen ground."

Emerson drew largely from the fountains of ancient Greece, but the distinct flavor of Oriental idealism pervades his thought. It were as if his thought had seeped up through the deep sands of Oriental thought, rising and filling a basin of the purest Greek design, from thence bubbling and pouring forth in a way distinctively his own.

In his conception of the One, Emerson is a Hindu; but in his expression of the Life of the Many, Emerson is filled with the true Greek spirit.

And this passed on to the New Thought—this strange mingling of the Orient and Ancient Greece—the calm, serene majesty of Brahm, and the leaping, joyous, living, loving, changing form of Pan. In the first aspect, we see Brahm the Unmanifest, brooding over his creations, breathing outward and inward, in aeonic rhythm, throughout all eternity. In the second, we see Pan, the expression of Manifest Life.

THE INFLUENCE OF THE NEW PSYCHOLOGY

The rise of Emerson's Transcendentalism was accompanied by an equally striking development of "The New Psychology." The peculiar features of this last named phase of thought were:

(1) the idea that the mind has a direct and positive effect upon the body; that physical conditions, in health and disease, depend materially upon mental states;

(2) that the mind possessed many latent powers which are capable of development and manifestation along lines running above the more common natural processes;

(3) that man, by the exercise of his will and imaging faculties, may transform his character and nature, and literally "make himself over."

These three principles were expounded by numerous teachers. A study of the writings along these lines, in the middle part of the nineteenth century gives an idea of the intense interest manifested in these subjects.

There was no apparent connection between them and the Transcendental Movement, except that as a rule the same persons were likely to be attracted toward both. But both movements were destined from the first to coalesce, blend together, and unite into one common and larger movement.

THE BLENDING OF TRASCENDENTALISM AND NEW PSYCHOLOGY

The first indication of the blending was the appearance of persons in various parts of the country, who were greatly successful in the healing of diseases by means of the methods of the New Psychology, based, however, on the fundamental principles of Transcendentalism.

The two streams united at this point, but just where or how it is almost impossible to state. But the union and blending is unmistakable—the waters of the two streams may be clearly distinguished as they are seen flowing, side by side, along the new channel.

And, here, as is always the case in new movements in which the healing element enters, the phase of healing for a time overbalanced and outshone the philosophical phase. It has been so in all new religions, and it was so in the new religio-philosophy, the New Thought. The people were first attracted by the promise of the healing of their bodily ills, and afterward remained to absorb the philosophy.

These mental healers were the first to make the natural connection between the transcendental philosophy of Emerson and his followers and the application of mind-power to the healing of disease. They did their work well, and others followed in the steps. Phineas Quimby, Horatio Dresser, Evans, and a few others are remembered—the others are forgotten. All served their purpose in the great plan, however, and made the connecting link between the two schools of thought.

The investigators of psycho-therapy in the ranks of the medical fraternity in France and other European countries, added new interest to the subject, and many physicians sought an explanation for the wonderful successes of the mind-healers in the new theories and methods of Suggestive Therapeutics. Writers began to publish magazine articles and books showing that diseases had been cured by mental methods, in all times and in all ages, regardless of special theories or doctrine.

This, however, did not discourage the new movement as intended, for its own writers soon pointed out that these ancient cures, as well as many modern ones, were made by reason of a great natural principle of Mind which many had stumbled upon and used in ignorance of its real nature. These discussions, however, served a useful purpose in informing the public that these strange cures were based upon perfectly natural, and not super-natural, principles; and that they did not depend upon any special creed or dogma for successful application. Accordingly, the workers in the independent field increased rapidly in number, and thousands of earnest persons who were cured helped to spread the tidings of the New Thought as it then began to be called the old term being given a new application.

The influence of Theosophy also must be taken into consideration when we look back over the history of New Thought.

While not adopting its doctrines, the New Thought found much in the new Theosophical teachings to corroborate their own ideas (since both schools drew freely from the same original ancient sources).

In the same way, the renewed interest in the teachings of certain sects of the Early Christian Church, brought to light many points of resemblance between some of the beliefs of the old Fathers of the Church and the New Thought teachings. This, also, was to be expected, in view of the fact that both teachings were largely influenced by Neo-Platonism.

The popular works of Prentice Mulford served to bring into still wider prominence that phase of the New Thought teaching which deals with the influence of the mind regarding one's environment, success, etc. His essay, "The Drawing Power of The Mind," opened a new world of thought to many. Many magazines devoted to the subject were published, and quite a number of books dealing with the question were written and circulated.

A new interest in the philosophies of the past and present was shown by a large portion of the public, and a marked increase in the production and sale of metaphysical books was noticed.

Gradually, but steadily, the interest of New Thought people extended to the spiritual phases of the philosophy, and to the phase of self-help and character-building, the healing phase, however, maintaining its original importance.

NEW THOUGHT AND RELIGION

Mrs. Eddy, the founder of Christian Science, undoubtedly did more than any other to make popular the healing of the body by metaphysical methods, and her insistence upon her basic philosophy was an inspiration to others who agreed with her in the main, but who differed from her regarding certain points of doctrine and organization.

The wonderful success of the Christian Science Church is an indication of the great interest in the new philosophy manifest on all sides. But the bulk of the New Thought following were not connected with any organization. Many were independents; many retained their relations with the orthodox churches.

Many of Mrs. Eddy's pupils separated from her organization, and formed schools of their own, or else practiced and taught independently. Others, not her pupils, but influenced by the movement which she has initiated, also founded similar organizations and associations. Many while retaining allegiance to the orthodox churches, nevertheless availed themselves of the benefits of mental or spiritual healing, their work being known as "faith healing," "mind-cure," "mental science," "divine science," etc. Differing widely regarding details of theory, all made cures and attracted a following. In New England, especially, the healing of disease by the power of the mind assumed the nature of a "fad," and became widely known as "the Boston craze."

The" Emmanuel Movement," which is really an application of certain New Thought principles, was instituted in certain churches, and thousands were healed thereby. The theology of the day was strongly influenced by the New Thought teachings, and the rapid face about noticed by all students of the Protestant Churches, is due almost entirely to this general spirit set into activity by the New Thought movement. Professor William James says:

"Those of us who are sexagenarians have witnessed in our own persons one of those gradual mutations of intellectual climate, due to innumerable influences, that make the thought of a past generation seem as foreign to its successor as if it were the expression of a different race of men. The theological machinery that spoke so livingly to our ancestors, with its finite age of the world, its creation out of nothing, its judicial morality and eschatology, its relish for rewards and punishments, its treatment of God as an external contriver, an 'intelligent and moral governor, ' sound as odd to most of us as if it were some outlandish savage religion . . .

The only opinion quite worthy of arresting our attention will fall within the general scope of what may roughly be called the pantheistic field of vision, the vision of God as the indwelling divine rather than the external creator, and of human life as part and parcel of that deep reality."

Prof. Charles W. Eliot, late President of Harvard, in his celebrated address on "The Religion of the Future," says:

"The New Thought of God will be its most characteristic element. This ideal will comprehend the Jewish Jehovah, the Christian Universal Father, the modern physicist's omnipresent and exhaustless Energy, and the biological conception of a Vital Force. The Infinite Spirit pervades the universe, just as the spirit of man pervades his body, and acts, consciously or unconsciously in every atom of it. The twentieth century will accept literally and implicitly St. Paul's statement, 'In Him we live, and move, and have our being.'

The new religion is therefore thoroughly monotheistic, its God being the one infinite force; but this one God is not withdrawn or removed, but indwelling and especially dwelling in every living creature . . . This central idea of a new religion will therefore be a humane and worthy idea of God, thoroughly consistent with the nineteenth century revelations concerning man and nature, and with all the tenderest and loveliest teachings which have come down to us from the past."

THE RISING OF OPTISMISM AND SELF-HELP

One of the most striking manifestations of the new spirit abroad in the land was the rise of the Spirit of Optimism.

People who never heard of the New Thought found themselves impressed with the importance of Being Cheerful, Looking on the Bright Side, and Keeping Sweet. "Don't "Worry" signs and motto-cards were noticed on all sides.

Also, **a new spirit of Self-Reliance and Self-help was manifested.**

Although there were many organizations created around beliefs contained in the New Thought, New Thought was never an organization-it was and is a MENTAL ATTITUDE.

Many manifest "New Thought" principles with success in their everyday lives—and yet do not realize that New Thought has had anything to do with their views. They have simply absorbed the New Thought spirit which surrounds them on all sides. The orthodox pulpits echo New Thought sermons every

Sunday, although the term is never mentioned—and this, too, is well, for New Thought is, and should be, as free as air, and the property of all.

THE MAIN TEACHINGS OF NEW THOUGHT

The following, expressed in many different forms, according to the views of the respective teachers, are the fundamental principles of The New Thought.

1. There is a Supreme Power back of, underlying, and in all things. It is Infinite, Illimitable, Eternal and Unchangeable. It IS, has always been, and always will be. It is Omnipresent (present everywhere); Omnipotent (all powerful, possessing all the power that is) ; and Omniscient (all-knowing, all-seeing, knowing everything, seeing everything). This Supreme Power— Universal Presence— All Mind—may be called MIND, SPIRIT, LAW, THE ABSOLUTE, FIRST CAUSE, NATURE, UNIVERSAL PRINCIPLE, LIFE, or whatever name best suits the taste of the person using the term, but call it what you will you mean this Supreme Power—the Centre. GOD is this great Universal Presence, and not the conception of a limited God held by any man. GOD must be illimitable, and all of the Universe must be an emanation of him

2. Humanity is unfolding in consciousness, and many have now reached that stage of spiritual consciousness whereby they become conscious of the existence and immanence of GOD, and thus know rather than entertain a belief based upon the authority, real or assumed, of other men. This God-consciousness to which humanity is rapidly tending, is the result of our unfoldment, development, and evolution for ages, and, when fully possessed by us, will completely

revolutionize our present conceptions of life, our ethics, customs, conditions and economics.

3. GOD is not a being afar off from us, full of wrath and punishment, but he is right here with us; all around us; even in us; understanding us from the beginning; realizing our limitations; full of love; and patiently seeing the gradual growth and unfoldment which brings us into a clearer understanding of him.

4. As to the reason of GOD'S plans and laws, The New Thought does not pretend to have knowledge, holding that this cannot be known by Man in his present stage of development, although by reason and intuition he is beginning to understand that all is Good, and to see evidences of a loving, good, perfect, just and wise plan, in all the experiences of life. And having that Intelligent Faith which comes of the God-consciousness, it rests content, saying "GOD IS —and all is well."

5. All is One—all the Universe, high and low, developed and undeveloped, manifest and unmanifest, is One— all is an emanation of GOD. Everything in the universe is in touch with every other thing, and all is in connection with the Centre— GOD. Every atom is a part of a mighty whole, and nothing can happen to any atom without a corresponding effect upon every other part of the whole. The sense of separateness is an illusion of the undeveloped consciousness, but an illusion necessary in certain stages for the working out of the plan. When we have so far progressed in spiritual growth and unfoldment that certain heretofore dormant faculties awaken to consciousness, or rather, when our consciousness has so far developed that it takes cognizance of certain

faculties the existence of which has heretofore been unknown to us, we becomes conscious of the Oneness of All, and our relation to all that is. It is not merely a matter of intellectual conception, it is the growth of a new consciousness. The person who possesses this, simply knows; the person who has it not, deems the idea allied to insanity. This Cosmic Knowing comes to many as an illumination; to others it is a matter of gradual and slow development.

6. We are Spiritual beings, our Soul is Immortal. New Thought teachers differ in their theories as to just how and where he will live in the future. However, when we obtain that wonderful assurance of immortality from our awakened spiritual faculties, we see no need of worrying about the "how" and "where". We know that *we are* and *will be*. We have within us such an abiding sense of existence, and deathlessness, that all of humanity's speculations seem like idle theories to us— useful in their place, of course, but of no vital importance to us. We know there are no limits to the possible manifestations of life— we know that "infinity plus infinity" would not begin to express the possibilities before us, and we fret not. We learn to live in the NOW, for we know that we are in Eternity right now, just as much as we ever will be, and we proceed to Live. We are concerned with Life, not with Death, and we Live. We have confidence in GOD and in the Divine Plan, and are content. We know that if our entire solar system, and every other system the suns of which are visible to us, were dissolved into their original elements, we would still exist, and would be still in the Universe. We know that the Universe is large, and that we are a part of it— that we cannot be

left out or banished from the Universe— that we are important atoms, and that our destruction would disarrange and destroy the whole. We know that while the Universe lasts— we last. That if we are destroyed the Universe is destroyed. We know that GOD had use for us or we would not be here, and we know that GOD makes no mistakes—changes not his mind— and destroys no soul that he has expressed. We say: we are Sons of GOD; what we shall be doth not yet appear; but come what will we are still Sons of GOD; what our future may be, concerns us not— it is not our business— we will place our hands in that of the Father and say "Lead Thou us on.".

7. Since we are immortal, Life can be seen only as being on an ascending scale, rising from lower to higher, and then on to higher and higher and higher. In the Universe there are beings much lower than us in the spiritual scale; and there are others much more advanced, much more highly developed than us, and we are progressing along the Path until some day we will be where they are; and others now much lower will someday be where we are now and so on.

8. There is a spiritual evolution going on in Humanity— we are growing, developing and unfolding in spiritual attainment. Our minds are developing and causing to unfold new faculties which will lead us to higher paths of attainment. The Higher Reason is beginning to make itself manifest. Humanity is nearing the plane of Cosmic Knowing.

9. *"Thoughts are things"*— every thought we think goes forth, carrying with it force which affects others to a greater or less extent, depending upon the force behind our thought, and the mental attitude of the

other persons. ***Like attracts like*** in the world of thought—we attract to ourselves thoughts in harmony with our own—people in harmony with our thoughts—,even things are influenced by thought in varying degrees.

10. "As a man thinketh in his heart so is he," and we may change, and often do change, our entire character and nature by a change of thoughts, an adjustment of mental attitude. Fearthought and Worry and all the rest of the foul brood of negative thoughts attract thoughts, people, things, from the outside, and pull us down to the level of our thought-pictures. On the contrary we may, by right thinking, raise ourselves from the mire, and surround with people and things corresponding to our thoughts. Thoughts take form in action.

11. The Mind is positive to the Body, and we may become sick or well —diseased or free from disease, according to our thoughts and mental attitude.

12. The Mind contains latent forces, lying dormant, awaiting the day of their unfoldment, which may be developed and trained and used in a wondrous way. We are in our infancy regarding the proper use of his mental powers.

This is only a little bit of the Truth. Every other man or woman has his or her bit, so that this portion is merely as a grain of sand on the seashore.

SOME OF THE GREATEST AUTHORS OF NEW THOUGHT

Among the early authors, we have Phineas Quimby (whose manuscripts were later edited and published by Horatio Dresser, son of one of Quimby's friends); Prentice Mulford (whose book "Your Forces and How to Use It", published in 6 volumes, influenced most of the next generation); and a little later on, Frank Channing Haddock.

The next generation started in the late 1890's early 1900's, and arrives to the middle 20's. Among them is Orison Swett Marden, whose influence in the self-help and self-reliance movement is paramount, with over 60 books. We also have William Walker Atkinson, whose 100+ books covered almost of areas of New Thought, including self-help and personal development, self-healing, and Eastern Philosophy.

Ralph Waldo Trine is considered the best seller of the New Thought writers, and he belong to the more Christian branch of the movement, but with a sort of "New Christianity", far away from dogmas and "churches", and more looking into the inner and real teachings of Jesus.

Judge Thomas Troward, who wrote at the end of the 19 century, beginning of the 20th, and his pupil, Genevieve Behrend, who wrote in the twenties, also belong to this so called Christian branch, although they call their movement "Mental Science".

In the middle, we find Wallace Wattles, who wrote self-help books ("the Science of Getting Rich", "The Science of Being Great); self-healing books and a beautiful Christian book -a New Christ-, with a vision of a more real Jesus, not the one sold by the churches.

We also find here Charles Haanel, with his Master Key System, and his Eastern Philosophy books like "The Amazing Secrets of the Yogi".

A third generation can be cited. They started writing in the 1920's and 1930's, and some keep writing until the 1960's. Very representative are Ernest Holmes (who cites as his biggest influence the writings of Ralph Waldo Trine), Christian D. Larson and Napoleon Hill (who thanks Haanel, Atkinson and Marden) the latter mostly on self-help and success; Larson and Holmes with a positive Christian self-help style.

ABOUT GENEVIEVE BEHREND

From 1912 to 1914, Genevieve Behrend focused on the wisdom and philosophy of Thomas Troward (1847- 1916), one of the most influential authors of the New Thought, whose compelling ideas provided much of the groundwork to its spiritual philosophy. As the discipline of "Mental science" was taking shape, Troward imparted his personal insight to only one pupil who could perpetuate this knowledge and share it with the world. She became his only personal student, something she declares, she attracted using the principles in Troward books. After her studies with Troward, Behrend began her mission in New York City where she established and ran The School of the Builders until 1925; and then established another school in Los Angeles. For the next 35 years she toured major cities throughout North America as a celebrated lecturer, teacher, and practitioner of "Mental Science".

BOOK TWO
YOUR INVISIBLE POWER

A Presentation of the Mental Science of Judge Thomas
Troward

Genevieve Behrend

FORWARD

THESE pages have been written for the purpose of furnishing you a key to the attainment of your desires, and to explain that Fear should be entirely banished from your consciousness in order for you to obtain possession of the things you want.

This presupposes, of course, that your desire for possession is based upon your aspiration for greater happiness. For example, you feel that the possession of more money, lands, or friends will make you happier, and your desire for possession of these things arises from a conviction that their possession will bring you freedom and contentment.

In your effort to possess, you will discover that the thing you most need is to consistently "Be" your best self.

One morning after class a man came to me and asked if I would speak the word of supply for him, as he was sadly in the need of money. He offered me a $5 bill with the remark: "Dear Madam, that is half of every dollar I have in the world. I am in debt; my wife and child have not the proper clothing; in fact, I must have money." I explained to him that money was the symbol of differentiated substance, that this substance filled all space, that it was present for him at that very moment, and would manifest to him as the money he required. "But," he questioned, "it may come too late." I told him it could not come too late, as it was eternally present. He understood and got the uplift of my spoken word.

I did not see the man again, but six months later I had a letter from him stating he was in New Orleans. He said, "I am well established here in my regular profession of photography; I own my own home, have an automobile of my own, and am generally prospering. And dear Mrs. Behrend, I want to thank you for lifting me out of the depths that day in New York.

Three days after I talked to you, a man whom I have not seen for years met me on the street. When I explained my situation to him, he loaned me the money to pay my bills and come down here. The enclosed check is to help you continue your wonderful work of teaching people how to mentally reach out and receive their never-failing supply. I would not take anything for my understanding as you have given it to me. God bless you."

A feeling that greater possessions, no matter of what kind they may be, will of themselves bring contentment or happiness, is a misunderstanding. No person, place, or thing can give you happiness. They may give you cause for happiness and a feeling of contentment, but the Joy of Living comes from within.

Therefore, it is here recommended that you should make the effort to obtain the things which you feel will bring you joy, provided that your desires are in accord with the Joy of Living.

It is also desired, in this volume, to suggest the possibilities in store for all who make persistent effort to understand the Law of Visualization, and who make practical application of this knowledge on whatever plane they may be. The word "effort," as here employed, is not intended to convey the idea of strain. All study and meditation should be without strain or tension.

It has been my endeavor to show that by starting at the beginning of the creative action, or mental picture, certain corresponding results are sure to follow. "While the laws of the Universe cannot be altered, they can be made to work under specific conditions, thereby producing results for individual advancement which cannot be obtained under the spontaneous workings of the law provided by Nature." However far these suggestions I have given —of the possibilities in store for you, through visualizing, may carry you beyond your past experience, they nowhere break the continuity of the law of cause and effect.

If through the suggestions here given, any one is brought to realize that his mind is a center through and in which "all power there is" is in operation, simply waiting to be given direction in the one and only way through which it can take specific action— and this means reaction in concrete or physical form—then the mission to which this book is dedicated has been fulfilled.

Try to remember that the picture you think, feel, and see is reflected into the Universal Mind, and by the natural law of reciprocal action must return to you in either spiritual or physical form. Knowledge of this law of reciprocal action between the individual and the Universal Mind opens to you free access to all you may wish to possess or to be.

It must be steadfastly borne in mind that all this can be true only for the individual who recognizes that he derives his power to make an abiding mental picture from the All-Originating Universal Spirit of Life, and can be used constructively only so long as it is employed and retained in harmony with the nature of the Spirit which originated it.

To insure this, there must be no inversion of the thought of the individual regarding his relationship to this Universal Originating Spirit, which is that of a son, through which the parent mind acts and reacts. Thus conditioned, whatever you think and feel yourself to be, the Creative Spirit of Life is bound to faithfully reproduce in a corresponding reaction.

This is the great reason for picturing yourself and your affairs the way you wish them to be as existing facts— though invisible to the physical eye—and living in your picture. An honest endeavor to do this, always recognizing that your own mind is a projection of the Originating Spirit, will prove to you that the best there is, is yours in all your ways.

G.B.

Los Angeles, California;
May, 1929.

1

Order of Visualization

THE exercise of the visualizing faculty keeps your mind in order, and attracts to you the things you need to make life more enjoyable in an orderly way.

If you train yourself in the practice of deliberately picturing your desire and carefully examining your picture, you will soon find that your thoughts and desires proceed in a more orderly procession than ever before.

Having reached a state of ordered mentality, you are no longer in a constant state of mental hurry. Hurry is Fear, and consequently destructive. In other words, when your understanding grasps the power to visualize your heart's desire and hold it with your will, it attracts to you all things requisite to the fulfillment of that picture by the harmonious vibrations of the law of attraction.

You realize that since Order is Heaven's first law, and visualization places things in their natural order, then it must be a heavenly thing to visualize. Everyone visualizes, whether he knows it or not. Visualizing is the great secret of success.

The conscious use of this great power attracts to you multiplied resources, intensifies your wisdom, and enables you to make use of advantages which you formerly failed to recognize.

A lady once came to me for help in selling a piece of property. After I explained to her just how to make a mental picture of the sale, going through the details mentally, exactly as she would do if the property were sold, she came a week later and told me how one day she was walking along the street, when the thought suddenly occurred to her to go and see a certain real estate dealer, to whom she had not yet been.

She hesitated for a moment when she first got the idea, as it seemed to her that that man could not sell her property. However, upon the strength of what I had told her, she followed the lead and went to the real estate man, who sold the property for her in just three days after she had first approached him. This was simply following along with the natural law of demand and supply.

We now fly through the air, not because anyone has been able to change the laws of Nature, but because the inventor of the flying machine learned how to apply Nature's laws and, by making orderly use of them, produced the desired result. So far as the natural forces are concerned, nothing has changed since the beginning. There were no airplanes in "the Year One," because those of that generation could not conceive the idea as a practical, working possibility. "It has not yet been done," was the argument, "and it cannot be done." Yet the laws and materials for practical flying machines existed then as now.

Troward tells us that the great lesson he learned from the airplane and wireless telegraphy is the triumph of principle over precedent, the working out of an idea to its logical conclusion in spite of accumulated contrary testimony of all past experience.

With such an example before you, you must realize that there are still greater secrets to be disclosed. Also, that you hold the key within yourself, with which to unlock the secret chamber that contains your heart's desire.

All that is necessary in order that you may use this key and make your life exactly what you wish it to be, is a careful inquiry into the unseen causes which stand back of every external and visible condition. Then bring these unseen causes into harmony with your conception, and you will find that you can make practical working realities of possibilities which at present seem but fantastic dreams."

A woman came to me in New York City, asking for help, as she was out of work. I spoke the word of ever-present supply for her and intensified it by mentally seeing the woman in the position she dreamed of, but which she had been unable to make a practical reality.

That same afternoon she telephoned and said she could hardly believe her senses, as she had just taken exactly the kind of a position she wanted. The employer told her she had been wanting a woman like her for months.

We all knew that the balloon was the forefather of the airplane. In 1766 Henry Cavendish, an English nobleman, proved that hydrogen gas was seven times lighter than air. From that discovery the balloon came into existence, and from the ordinary balloon the dirigible, a cigar-shaped airship, was evolved.

Study of aeronautics and laws of the aerial locomotion of birds and projectiles led to the belief that mechanism could be evolved by which heavier-than-air machines could be made to travel from place to place and remain in the air by the maintenance of great speed, which would overcome by propulsive force the ordinary law of gravitation. Professor Langley of Washington, who developed much of the theory which others afterward improved upon, was subjected to much derision when he sent a model airplane up, only to have it bury its nose in the muddy waters of the Potomac.

But the Wright Brothers, who experimented later, realized the possibility of traveling through the air in a machine that had no gas bag. They saw themselves enjoying this mode of transportation with great facility. It is said that one of the brothers would tell the other, when their varied experiences did not turn out as they expected: "It's all right, Brother, I can see myself riding in that machine, and it travels easily and steadily."

Those Wright Brothers knew what they wanted and kept their pictures constantly before them. Now transportation through the air is developing rapidly and we all feel sure it will in the near future become as ordinary a method of travel as the automobile.

In visualizing, or making a mental picture, you are not endeavoring to change the laws of Nature. You are fulfilling them.

Your object in visualizing is to bring things into regular order, both mentally and physically. When you realize that this method of employing the Creative Power brings your desires, one after another, into practical, material accomplishment, your confidence in the mysterious but unfailing law of attraction, which has its central power station in the very heart of your word-picture, becomes supreme. Nothing can shake it. You never feel that it is necessary to take anything from anybody else. You have learned that asking and seeking have, as their correlatives, receiving and finding. You know that all you have to do is to start the plastic substance of the Universe flowing into the thought-moulds your picture-desire provides.

2

How to Attract To Yourself The Things You Desire

THE power within you which enables you to form a thought-picture is the starting point of all there is. In its original state it is the undifferentiated formless substance of life. Your thought-picture makes the model, so to say, into which this formless substance takes shape.

Visualizing, or mentally seeing things and conditions as you wish them to be, is the condensing, the specializing power in you which might be illustrated by comparison with the lens of a magic lantern, which is one of the best symbols of the imaging faculty.

It illustrates the idea of the working of the Creative Spirit on the plane of initiative and selection—or in its concentrated, specializing form —in a remarkably clear manner. The picture slide illustrates your own mental picture—invisible in the lantern of your mind until you turn on the light of your will.

That is to say, you light up your desire with absolute faith that the Creative Spirit of Life, in you, is doing the work. By the steady flow of the light of the Will on the Spirit, your desired picture is projected upon the screen of the physical world—an exact reproduction of the pictured slide in your mind.

A woman came to me for help to cause her husband to return to her. She said she was very unhappy and lonely without him and longed to be reunited. I told her she could not lose love and protection, because both belonged to her. She asked what she should do to get her husband back again. I told her to follow the great power of intuition and think of her husband as perfectly free, and the embodiment of all that a husband should be.

She went away quite happy, but returned in a few days to tell me that her husband desired a divorce in order to marry again. She was quite agitated and had evidently relaxed her will in following the instructions given at the former interview. Again I told her to hold constantly in her mind that the loving protection of the Spirit of Life would guide her in perfect happiness.

A month later she came again and said that her husband had married the other woman. This time she had completely lost her mental grip. I repeated the words for her as before, and she regained her poise. Two months later she came back to me, full of joy. Her husband had come to her, begging her forgiveness, and telling her what a terrible mistake he had made, as he could not be happy without her. They are now living happily together and she, at least, learned the necessity of holding her pictured desire steadily in place by the use of her will.

Visualizing without a will sufficiently steady to inhibit every thought and feeling contrary to your pictured thought would be as useless as a magic lantern without the light.

On the other hand, if your will is sufficiently developed to bold your picture in thought and feeling, without any "ifs"; simply realizing that your thought is the great attracting power, then your mental picture is as certain to be projected upon your physical world as a picture slide put into a magic lantern shows on the screen. Try projecting the picture in a magic lantern with a light that is constantly shifting from one side to the other, and you will produce the effect of an uncertain will. It is as necessary that you should always have back of your picture a strong, steady will, as it is to have a strong steady light back of a picture slide.

The joyous assurance with which you make your picture is the very powerful magnet of Faith, and nothing can obliterate it. You are happier than you ever were, because you have learned to know where your source of supply is, and you rely upon its never-failing response to the direction you give it.

All said and done, happiness is the one thing which every human being wants, and the study of visualization enables you to get more out of life than you ever enjoyed before. Increasing possibilities keep opening out, more and more, before you.

A business man once told me that since practicing visualization, and forming the habit of devoting a few minutes each day to thinking about his work as he desired it to be, in a large, broad way, his orders had more than doubled in six months.

His method was to go into a room every morning before breakfast and take a mental inventory of his business as he had left it the evening before, and then enlarge upon it. He said he expanded and expanded in this way, until his affairs were in a remarkably successful condition. He would see himself in his office doing everything he wanted done. His occupation required him to meet many strangers every day.

In his mental picture he saw himself meeting these people, understanding their needs, and supplying them in just the way they wished. This habit, he said, had strengthened and steadied his will in an almost inconceivable manner.

Furthermore, by thus mentally seeing things as he wished them to be, he had acquired the confident feeling that a certain Creative Power was exercising itself, for him and through him, for the purpose of improving his little world.

When you first begin to visualize seriously, you may feel, as many others do, that someone else may be forming the same picture you are, and that, naturally, would not suit your purpose. Do not give yourself any concern about this.

Simply try to realize that your picture is an orderly exercise of the Universal Creative Power specifically applied. Then you may be sure that no one can work in opposition to you. The universal law of harmony prevents that.

Endeavor to bear in mind that your mental picture is Universal Mind specifically exercising its inherent powers of initiative and selection. God, or Universal Mind, made man for the special purpose of differentiating Himself through him. Everything there is, came into existence in this same way, by this self-same law of self-differentiation, and for the same purpose. First came the idea, the mental picture, or the prototype of the thing, which is the thing itself in its incipiency. The Great Architect of the Universe contemplated Himself as manifesting through his polar opposite—matter—and the idea expanded and projected itself until we have not only a world, but many worlds.

Many people ask, "But why should we have a physical world at all?" The answer is: "Because it is the nature of Originating Substance to solidify, under directivity rather than activity, just as it is the nature of wax to harden when it becomes cold, or plaster of Paris to become firm and solid when exposed to the air.

Your picture is this same Divine Substance in its original state, taking form through the individualized center of Divine operation, in your mind; and there is no power to prevent this combination of Spiritual Substance from becoming physical form. It is the nature of Spirit to complete its work, and an idea is not complete until it has made for itself a vehicle.

Nothing can prevent your picture from coming into concrete form except the same power which gave it birth—yourself.

Suppose you wish to have a more orderly room. You look about your room, and the idea of order suggests boxes, closets, shelves, hooks, and so forth. The box, the closet and the hooks, are all concrete ideas of order, because they are the vehicles through which order and harmony suggest themselves.

3

Relation between Mental and Physical Form

SOME persons feel that it is not quite proper to visualize for things. "It's too material," they say. Why, material form is necessary for the self-recognition of Spirit from the individual standpoint, and this is the means through which the Creative Process is carried forward.

Therefore, far from matter being an illusion and something which ought not to be, matter is the necessary channel for the selfdifferentiation of Spirit.

However, it is not my desire to lead you into lengthy and tiresome scientific reasoning, in order to remove the mystery from visualization and to put it upon a logical foundation.

Naturally, each individual will do this in his own way. My only wish is to point out to you the easiest way I know, which is the road on which Troward guides me. I feel sure you will conclude, as I have, that the only mystery in connection with visualizing is the mystery of life taking form, governed by unchangeable and easily understood laws.

We all possess more power and greater possibilities than we realize, and visualizing is one of the greatest of these powers, it brings other Possibilities to our observation. When we pause to think for a moment, we realize that for a cosmos to exist at all, it must be the outcome of a Cosmic Mind, which binds "all individual minds to a certain generic unity of action, thereby producing all things as realities and nothing as illusions."

If you will take this thought of Troward's and meditate upon it without prejudice, you will surely realize that concrete material form is an absolute necessity of the Creative Process; also "that matter is not an illusion but a necessary channel thru which life differentiates itself." If you consider matter in its right order, as the polar opposite to Spirit, you will not find any antagonism between them. On the contrary, together they constitute one harmonious whole. And when you realize this, you feel, in your practice of visualizing, that you are working from cause to effect, from beginning to end.

In reality your mental picture is the specialized outworking of the Originating Spirit. One could talk for hours on purely scientific lines, showing, as Troward says, "that raw material for the formation of the solar systems is universally distributed throughout all space. Yet investigation shows that while the Heavens are studded with millions of suns, there are spaces which show no signs of cosmic activity. This being true, there must be something which started cosmic activity in certain places, while passing over others in which the raw material was equally available. At first thought, one might attribute development of cosmic energy to the etheric particles themselves. Upon investigation however, we find that this is mathematically impossible in a medium which is equally distributed throughout space, for all its particles are in equilibrium; therefore, no one particle possesses in itself a greater power of originating motion than the other. Thus we find that the initial movement, though working in and through the particles of primary substance, is not the particles themselves. It is this something we mean when we speak of Spirit."

This same power that brought universal substance into existence will bring your individual thought or mental picture into physical form. There is no difference in the power. The only difference is a difference of degree. The power and the substance themselves are the same. Only in working out your mental picture, it has transferred its creative energy from the Universal to the particular, and is working in the same unfailing manner from its specific center, your mind.

4

Operation of Your Mental Picture

THE operation of a large telephone system may be used as a simile. The main, or head central subdivides itself into many branch centrals, every branch being in direct connection with the main central, and each individual branch recognizing the source of its existence, reports all things to its central head. Therefore, when assistance of any nature is required: new supplies, difficult repairs to be done, or what not, the branch in need goes at once to its central head. It would not think of referring its difficulties (or its successes) to the main central of a telegraph system, though they might belong to the same organization. These different branch centrals know that the only remedy for any difficulty must come from the central out of which they were projected and to which they are always attached.

If we, as individual branches of the Universal Mind, would refer our difficulties in the same confident manner to the source from which we were projected, and use the remedies which it has provided, we would realize what Jesus meant when he said, "Ask and ye shall receive." Our every requirement would be met. Surely the Father must supply the child. The trunk of the tree cannot fail to provide for its branches.

A man came to me in great distress, saying he was about to lose his home in the South. In his own words, it was mortgaged to the hilt, and his creditors were going to foreclose. It was the house in which he had been born and had grown to young manhood, and the thought of losing it filled his heart and mind with sorrow, not only from a money standpoint, but from the standpoint of sentimental association.

I explained to him that the Power that brought him into existence did so for the purpose of expressing its limitless supply through him; that there was no power on earth which could cut him off from his source except his own consciousness, and that in reality he would not be cut off then. I explained to him that he had it, but was unable to recognize that it was there, and said to him, "Infinite substance is manifesting in you right now."

The next week, on Sunday, just before leaving my dressing room in the Selwyn Theatre to give my afternoon message, I received the following note:

"Dear Mrs. Behrend: I want you to know that I am the happiest man in the whole city of New York. My home in the South is saved. The money came in the most miraculous way, and I have telegraphed enough to pay off the mortgage. Please tell the people this afternoon about this wonderful Power."

You may be sure I did, explaining to them that everything animate or inanimate is called into existence or outstandingness by a Power which itself does not stand out. The Power which creates the mental picture—the Originating Spirit Substance of your pictured desire—does not stand out. It projects the substance of itself, which is a solidified counterpart of itself, while it—the Power—remains invisible to the physical eye. Those will appreciate the value of visualizing who are able to realize Paul's meaning when he said, "The worlds were formed by the word of God. Things which are seen are not made of things which do appear."

There is nothing unusual or mysterious in the idea of your pictured desire coming into material evidence. It is the working of a universal, natural Law. The world was projected by the selfcontemplation of the Universal Mind, and this same action is taking place in its individualized branch which is the Mind of Man. Everything in the whole world, from the hat on your head to the boots on your feet, has its beginning in mind and comes into existence in exactly the same manner. All are projected thoughts, solidified. Your personal advance in evolution depends on your right use of the power of visualizing, and your use of it depends on whether you recognize that you, yourself, are a particular center through and in which the Originating Spirit is finding ever new expression for potentialities already existing within Itself. This is evolution.

Your mental picture is the force of attraction which evolves and combines the Originating Substance into specific shape. Your picture is the combining and evolving power house, in a generative sense, so to say, through which the Originating Creative Spirit expresses itself. Its creative action is limitless, without beginning and without end, and always progressive and orderly. "It proceeds stage by stage, each stage being a necessary preparation for the one to follow."

Now let us see if we can get an idea of the different stages by which the things in the world have come to be.

Troward says, "If we can get at the working principle which is producing these results, we can very quickly and easily give it personal application. First, we find that the thought of Originating Life, or Spirit, concerning Itself is its simple awareness of its own being, and this, demanding a relationship to something else, produces a primary ether, a universal substance out of which everything in the world must grow."

Troward also tells us that "though this awareness of being is a necessary foundation for any further possibilities, it is not much to talk about." It is the same with individualized Spirit, which is yourself.

Before you can entertain the idea of making a mental picture of your desire as being at all practical, you must have some idea of your being; of your "I am"; and just as soon as you are conscious of your "I am"-ness, you begin to wish to enjoy the freedom which this consciousness suggests. You want to do more and be more, and as you fulfill this desire within yourself, localized spirit begins conscious activities in you. The thing you are more concerned with is the specific action of the Creative Spirit of Life, Universal Mind specialized. The localized God-germ in you~ is your personality, your individuality and since the joy of absolute freedom is the inherent nature of this God-germ, it is natural that it should endeavor to enjoy itself through its specific center. And as you grow in the comprehension that your being, your individuality, is God particularizing Himself, you naturally develop Divine tendencies. You want to enjoy life and liberty. You want freedom in your affairs as well as in your consciousness, and it is natural that you should.

With this progressive wish there is always a faint thought-picture. As your wish and your recognition grow into an intense desire, this desire becomes a clear mental picture. For example, a young lady studying music wishes she had a piano in order to practice at home. She wants the piano so much that she can mentally see it in one of the rooms. She holds the picture of the piano and indulges in the mental reflection of the pleasure and advantage it will be to have the piano in the corner of the living room. One day she finds it there, just as she had pictured it.

As you grow in understanding as to who you are, where you came from, what the purpose of your being is, and how you are to fulfill the purpose for which you are intended, you will become a more and more perfect center through which the Creative Spirit of Life can enjoy itself. And you will realize that there can be but one creative process filling all space, which is the same in its potentiality whether universal or individual. Furthermore, all there is, whether on the plane of the visible or invisible, had its origin in the localized action of thought, or a mental picture, and this includes yourself, because you are Universal Spirit localized, and the same creative action is taking place through you.

Now you are no doubt asking yourself why there is so much sickness and misery in the world. If the same power and intelligence which brought the world into existence is in operation in the mind of man, why does it not manifest itself as strength joy, health and plenty? If one can have one's desires fulfilled by simply making a mental picture of that desire, holding on to it with the will, and without anxiety, doing on the outward plane whatever seems necessary to bring the desire into fulfillment, then there seems no reason for the existence of sickness and poverty. Surely no one desires either.

The first reason is that few persons will take the trouble to inquire into the working principle of the Laws of Life. If they did, they would soon convince themselves that there is no necessity for the sickness and poverty which we see about us. They would realize that visualizing is a principle and not a fallacy. There are a few who have found it worthwhile to study this simple, though absolutely unfailing law, which will deliver them from bondage. However, the race as a whole is not willing to give the time required for the study. It is either too simple, or too difficult. They may make a picture of their desire with some little understanding of visualizing for a day or two, but more frequently it is for an hour or so.

If you will insist upon mentally seeing yourself surrounded by things and conditions as you wish them to be you will understand that the Creative Energy sends its substance in the direction indicated by the tendency of your thoughts. Herein lies the advantage of holding your thought in the form of a mental picture.

A man in the hardware business in New Jersey came to me in great distress. He would have to go into bankruptcy unless something happened in a fortnight. He said he had never heard of visualizing. I explained to him how to make a mental picture of his business increasing, instead of a picture of losing it. In about a month's time he returned very happy and told me how he had succeeded. He said, "I have my debts all paid, and my shop is full of new supplies." His business was then on a solid basis. It was beautiful to see his Faith.

The more enthusiasm and faith you are able to put into your picture, the more quickly it will come into visible form, and your enthusiasm is increased by keeping your desire secret. The moment you speak it to any living soul, that moment your power is weakened. Your power, your magnet of attraction is not that strong, and consequently cannot reach so far. The more perfectly a secret between your mind and your outer self is guarded, the more vitality you give your power of attraction. One tells one's troubles to weaken them, to get them off one's mind, and when a thought is given out, its power is dissipated. Talk it over with yourself, and even write it down, then destroy the paper.

However, this does not mean that you should strenuously endeavor to compel the Power to work out your picture on the special lines that you think it should. That method would soon exhaust you and hinder the fulfillment of your purpose. A wealthy relative need not necessarily die, or someone lose a fortune on the street, to materialize the $10,000 which you are mentally picturing.

One of the doormen in the building in which I lived heard much of the mental picturing of desires from visitors passing out of my rooms. The average desire was for $500. He considered that five dollars was more in his line and began to visualize it, without the slightest idea of where or how he was to get it. My parrot flew out of the window, and I telephoned to the men in the courtyard to get it for me. One caught it, and it bit him on the finger. The doorman, who had gloves on, and did not fear a similar hurt, took hold of it and brought it up to me. I gave him five one-dollar bills for his service. This sudden reward surprised him. He enthusiastically told me that he had been visualizing for just $5, merely from hearing that others visualized. He was delighted at the unexpected realization of his mental picture.

All you have to do is to make such a mental picture of your heart's desire, and hold it cheerfully in place with your will, always conscious that the same Infinite Power which brought the universe into existence brought you into form for the purpose of enjoying Itself in and through you. And since it is all Life, Love, Light, Power, Peace, Beauty, and Joy, and is the only Creative Power there is, the form it takes in and through you depends upon the direction given it by your thought. In you it is undifferentiated, waiting to take any direction given it as it passes through the instrument which it has made for the purpose of self-distribution—you.

It is this Power which enables you to transfer your thoughts from one form to another. The power to change your mind is the individualized Universal

Power taking the initiative, giving direction to the unformed substance contained in every thought. It is the simplest thing in the world to give this highly sensitive Substance any form you will, through visualizing. Anyone can do it with a small expenditure of effort.

Once you really believe that your mind is a center through which the unformed substance of all there is in your world, takes involuntary form, the only reason your picture does not always materialize is because you have introduced something antagonistic to the fundamental principle. Very often this destructive element is caused by the frequency with which you change your pictures. After many such changes, you decide that your original desire is what you want after all. Upon this conclusion, you begin to wonder why it (being your first picture) has not materialized.

The Substance with which you are mentally dealing is more sensitive than the most sensitive photographer's film. If, while taking a picture, you suddenly remembered you had already taken a picture on that same plate, you would not expect a perfect result of either picture. On the other hand, you may have taken two pictures on the same plate unconsciously. When the plate has been developed, and the picture comes into physical view, you do not condemn the principle of photography, nor are you puzzled to understand why your picture has turned out so unsatisfactorily. You do not feel that it is impossible for you to obtain a good, clear picture of the subject in question. You know that you can do so, by simply starting at the beginning, putting in a new plate, and determining to be more careful while taking your picture next time. If these lines are followed out, you are sure of a satisfactory result. If you will proceed in the same manner with your mental picture, doing your part in a correspondingly confident frame of mind, the result will be just as perfect. The laws of visualizing are as infallible as the laws governing photography. In fact, photography is the outcome of visualizing.

Again, your results in visualizing the fulfillment of your desires may be imperfect, and your desires delayed, through the misuse of this power, owing to the thought that the fulfillment of your desire is contingent upon certain persons or conditions. The Originating Principle is not in any way dependent upon any person, place, or thing. It has no past and knows no future. The law is that the Originating Creative Principle of Life is "the universal here and everlasting now." It creates its own vehicles through which to operate. Therefore, past experience has no bearing upon your present picture. So do not try to obtain your desire through a channel which may not be natural for it, even though it may seem reasonable to you. Your feeling should be that the thing, or the consciousness, which you so much desire, is normal and natural, a part of yourself, a form of your evolution. If you can do this, there is no power to prevent your enjoying the fulfillment of the picture you have in mind, or any other you may create.

5

Expressions from Beginners

HUNDREDS of persons have realized that "visualizing is an Aladdin's lamp to him with a mighty will." General Foch says that his feelings were so outraged during the Franco-Prussian war in 1870 that he visualized himself leading a French army against the Germans to victory. He said he made his picture, smoked his pipe, and waited. This is one result of visualizing with which we are all familiar.

A famous actress wrote a long article in one of the leading Sunday papers last winter, describing how she rid herself of excessive avoirdupois by seeing her figure constantly as she wished to be.

A very interesting letter came to me from a doctor's wife, while I was lecturing in New York. She began with the hope that I would never discontinue my lectures on visualization, which were helping humanity to realize the wonderful fact that they possessed the means of liberation within themselves. Relating her own experience, she said that she was born on the East Side of New York in the poorest quarter. From earliest girlhood she had cherished a dream of marrying a physician someday. This dream gradually formed a stationary mental picture. The first position she obtained was in the capacity of a maid in a physician's family. Leaving this place, she entered the family of another doctor. The wife of her employer died, and the doctor married her — the result of long-pictured yearning. After that, both she and her husband conceived the idea of owning a fruit farm in the South. They formed a mental picture of the idea and put their faith in its eventual fulfillment. The letter she sent me came from her fruit farm in the South. Her second mental picture had seen the light of materialization.

Many letters of a similar nature come to me every day. The following is a case that was printed in the New York Herald last May: "Atlantic City, May 5— She was an old woman, and when she was arraigned before Judge Clarence Goldenberg in the police court today she was so weak and tired she could hardly stand. The Judge asked the court attendant what she was charged with.

'Stealing a bottle of milk, Your Honor,' repeated the officer. 'She took it from the doorstep of a downtown cottage before daybreak this morning.'

'Why did you do that?' Judge Goldenberg asked her.

'I was hungry,' said the old lady.

'Well, you're not very wealthy now, but you're no longer poor. I've been searching for you for months. I've got $500 belonging to you from the estate of a relative. I am the executor of the estate.'

"Judge Goldenberg paid the woman's fine out of his own pocket, and then escorted her into his office, where he turned her legacy over to her and sent a policeman out to find her a lodging place."

I learned later that this little woman had been desiring and mentally picturing $500, while all the time ignorant of how it could possibly come to her. But she kept her vision and strengthened it with her faith.

In an issue of Good Housekeeping there was an article by Addington Bruce entitled "Stiffening Your Mental Backbone." It is very instructive, and would benefit anyone to read it. He says, in part: "Form the habit of devoting a few moments every day to thinking about your work in a large, broad, imaginative way, as a vital necessity to yourself and a useful service to society."

James J. Hill, the great railway magnate, before he started building his road from coast to coast, said that he took hundreds of trips all along the line before there was a rail laid. It is said that he would sit for hours with a map of the United States before him and mentally travel from coast to coast, just as we do now over his fulfilled mental picture. It would be possible to call your attention to hundreds of similar cases.

The method of picturing to yourself what you desire is both simple and enjoyable, if you once understand the principle back of it well enough to believe it. Over and above everything else, be sure of what it is you really want. Then specialize your desire along the lines given in the following chapter.

6

Suggestions for Making Your Mental Picture

PERHAPS you want to feel that you've lived to some purpose. You want to be contented and happy; you feel that good health and a successful business would give you contentment. After you have decided once and for all that this is what you want, you proceed to picture yourself healthy, and your business just as great a success as you can naturally conceive it growing into. The best times for making your definite picture are just before breakfast, and again, before retiring at night. As it is necessary to give yourself plenty of time, it may be necessary to rise earlier than you usually do. Go into a room where you will not be disturbed, meditate for a few moments upon the practical working of the law of visualizing, and ask yourself, "How did the things about me first come into existence? How can I get more quickly in touch with my invisible supply?"

Someone felt that comfort would be better expressed and experienced by sitting on a chair than on the floor. So the very beginning of a chair was the desire to be at ease. With this came the picture of some sort of a chair. The same principle applies to the hat and the clothes you wear. Go carefully into the thought of the principle back of the thing. Establish it as a personal experience; make it a fact to your consciousness.

Then open a window, take about ten deep breaths, and during the time draw a large imaginary circle of light pound you. As you inhale—keeping yourself in the center of this circle of light-— see great rays of light coming from the circle and entering your body at all points, centralizing itself at your solar plexus. Hold the breath a few moments at this central point of your body—the solar plexus— then slowly exhale. As you do this, mentally see imaginary rays, or sprays, of light going up through the body, and down and out through feet. Mentally spray your entire body with this imaginary light. When you have finished the breathing exercise, sit in a comfortable upright chair and mentally know there is but one Life, one Substance, and this Life Substance of the Universe is finding pleasure in self-recognition in you. Repeat some affirmation of this kind, until you feel the truth and stimulating reality of the words which you are affirming. Then begin your picture. If you are thorough in this, you will find yourself in the deep consciousness beneath the surface of your own thought power.

Whether your desire is for a state of consciousness, or a possession, large or small, begin at the beginning. If you want a house, begin by seeing yourself in the kind of house you desire. Go all through it, taking careful note of the rooms, where the windows are situated, and such other details as help you to feel the reality of your picture. You might change some of the furniture about and look into some of the mirrors just to see how healthy, wealthy, and happy you look. Go over your picture again and again, until you feel the reality of it, then write it all down just as you have seen it, with the feeling that:

"The best there is, is mine. There is no limit to me, because my mind is a center of divine operation," and your picture is as certain to come true, in your physical world, as the sun is to shine.

7

Things to Remember

In Using Your Thought Power for the Production of New Conditions

1. Be sure to know exactly what conditions you wish to produce. Then weigh carefully what further results the accomplishment of your desire will lead to.

2. By letting your thought dwell upon a mental picture, you are concentrating the Creative Action of Spirit in this center, where its forces are equally balanced.

3. Visualizing brings your objective mind into a state of equilibrium, which enables you to consciously direct the flow of Spirit to a definitely recognized purpose, and to carefully guard your thoughts from including a flow in the opposite direction.

4. You must always bear in mind that you are dealing with a wonderful potential energy, which is not yet differentiated into any particular form, and that by the action of your mind, you can differentiate it into any specific form that you will. Your picture assists you to keep your mind fixed on the fact that the inflow of this Creative Energy is taking place. Also, by your mental picture, you are determining the direction you wish the sensitive Creative Power to take, and by doing this, you make the externalization of your picture a certainty.

5. Remember when you are visualizing properly that there is no strenuous effort to hold your thought-forms in place. Strenuous effort defeats your purpose, and suggests the consciousness of an adverse force to be fought against, and this creates conditions adverse to your picture.

6. By holding your picture in a cheerful frame of mind, you shut out all thoughts that would disperse or dissipate the spiritual nucleus of your picture. Because the law is Creative in its action, your pictured desire is certain of accomplishment.

7. The seventh and great thing to remember in visualizing is that you are making a mental picture for the purpose of determining the quality you are giving to the previously undifferentiated substance and energy, rather than to arrange the specific circumstances for its manifestation. That is the work of Creative Power itself. It will build its own forms of expression quite naturally, if you will allow it, and save you a great deal of needless anxiety. What you really want is expansion in a certain direction, whether of health, wealth or what not, and so long as you get it—as you surely will, if you confidently hold to your picture—what does it matter whether it reaches by some channel which you thought you could count upon, or through some other of whose existence you had no idea. You are concentrating energy of a particular kind for a particular purpose. Keep this in mind and let specific details take care of themselves, and never mention what you are doing to anyone.

Remember always, that "Nature, from her clearly visible surface to her most arcane depths, is one vast storehouse of light and good entirely devoted to your individual use." Your conscious Oneness with the great Whole is the secret of success, and when once you have fathomed this, you can enjoy your possession of the whole, or a part of it, at will, because by your recognition you have made it, and can increasingly make it, yours.

Never forget that every physical thing, whether for you or against you, was a sustained thought before it was a thing. Thought, as thought, is neither good nor bad; it is Creative Action and always takes physical form. Therefore, the thoughts you dwell upon become the things you possess or do not possess.

A man came to me telling me how he longed to marry a certain young woman, but felt he could not afford to as his salary was small, and work uncertain. I spoke the word of ever-present Certain, Unlimited Supply and explained that Love knows no failure.

"It is yours to enjoy. See yourself in the kind of a home you both want. Do your part, keep on loving the girl, and believe absolutely in that which Lives and Loves in you."

A few months later they both came to my study looking radiantly happy. I knew they were married. The wife said to me: "Dear Mrs. Behrend, we are very happy because we now know how to use our thought power and hold our consciousness as one, with all we want."

So be yourself and enjoy Life in your own Divine way. Do not fear to be your true self, for everything you want, wants you.

8

Why I Took Up the Study of Mental Science

I HAVE frequently been questioned about my reasons for taking up the study of Mental Science, and as to the results of my search, not only in the knowledge of principles, but also in the application of that knowledge for the development of my own life.

Such inquiries are justifiable, because one who essays the role of a messenger of psychological truths can only be convincing as he or she has tested them in the laboratory of personal mental experience. This is particularly true in my case, as the only personal pupil of Judge Troward, the great Master in Mental Science, whose teaching is based upon the relation borne by the Individual Mind toward the Universal Creative Mind, which is the Giver of Life, and the manner in which that relation may be invoked to secure expansion and fuller expression in the individual life.

My initial impulse toward the study of Mental Science was an overwhelming sense of loneliness. In every life there must come some such experience of spiritual isolation as pervaded my life at that period. Notwithstanding the fact that each day found me in the midst of friends, surrounded by mirth and gaiety, there was a persistent feeling that I was alone in the world. I had been a widow for about three years, wandering from country to country, seeking for peace of mind.

The circumstances and surroundings of my life were such that my friends looked upon me as an unusually fortunate young woman. Although they recognized that I had sustained a great loss when my husband died, they knew that he had left me well provided for, free to go anywhere my pleasure dictated.

Yet, if my friends could have penetrated my inmost emotions, they would have found a deep sense of emptiness and isolation. This feeling inspired a spirit of unrest, which drove me on and on in fruitless search upon the outside, for that which I later learned could only be found within.

I studied Christian Science, but it gave me no solace, though fully realizing the great work the Scientists were doing, and even having the pleasure and privilege of meeting Mrs. Eddy personally. But it was impossible for me to accept the fundamental teachings of Christian Science and make practical application of it.

When about to abandon the search for contentment and resign myself to resume a life of apparent amusement, a friend invited me to visit the great Seer and Teacher, Abdul Baha. After my interview with this most wonderful of men, my search for contentment began to take a change. He had told me that I would travel the world over seeking the truth, and when I had found it, would speak it out. The fulfillment of the statement of this Great Seer then seemed to be impossible. But it carried a measure of encouragement, and at least indicated that my former seeking had been in the wrong direction. I began in a feeble groping way to find contentment within myself, for had he not intimated that I should find the truth? That was the big thing, and about the only thing I remember of our interview.

A few days later, upon visiting the office of a New Thought practitioner, my attention was attracted to a book on his table entitled "The Edinburgh Lectures on Mental Science," by T. Troward. It interested me to see that Troward was a retired Divisional Judge from the Punjab, India. I purchased the book, thinking I would read it through that evening. Many have endeavored to do the same thing, only to find, as I did, that the book must be studied in order to be understood, and hundreds have decided, just as I did, to give it their undivided attention. After finding this treasure book, I went to the country for a few days, and while there, studied the volume as thoroughly as I could.

It seemed extremely difficult, and I decided to purchase another book of Troward 's, in the hope that its study might not require so much of an effort. Upon inquiry I was told that a subsequent volume, "The Dore Lectures," was much the simpler and better of the two books. When I procured it, I found that it must also be studied. It took me weeks and months to get even a vague conception of the meaning of the first chapter of Dore, which is entitled "Entering Into the Spirit of It." I mean by this that it took me months to enter into the spirit of what I was reading.

But in the meantime a paragraph from page 26 arrested my attention, as seeming the greatest thing I had ever read. I memorized it and endeavored with all my soul to enter into the spirit of Troward's words. The paragraph reads:

"My mind is a center of Divine operation. The Divine operation is always for expansion and fuller expression, and this means the production of something beyond what has gone before, something entirely new, not included in the past experience, though proceeding out of it by an orderly sequence or growth. Therefore, since the Divine cannot change its inherent nature, it must operate in the same manner with me; consequently, in my own special world, of which I am the center, it will move forward to produce new conditions, always in advance of any that have gone before."

It took an effort on my part to memorize this paragraph, but in the endeavor toward this end, the words seemed to carry with them a certain stimulus. Each repetition of the paragraph made it easier for me to enter into the spirit of it. The words expressed exactly what I had been seeking for. My one desire was for peace of mind. I found it comforting believe that the Divine operation in me could expand to fuller expression and produce more and more contentment— in fact, a peace mind and a degree of contentment greater than I had ever known. The paragraph further inspired me with deep interest to feel that the life-spark in me could bring into my life something entirely new. I did not wish to obliterate my past experience, but that was exactly what Troward said it would not do. The Divine operation would not exclude my past experience, but proceeding out of it would bring some new things that would transcend anything that I had ever experienced before.

Meditation on these statements brought with it a certain joyous feeling. What a wonderful thing it would be if I could accept and sincerely believe, beyond all doubt, that this one statement of Troward's was true. Surely the Divine could not change its inherent nature, and since Divine life is operating in me, I must be Divinely inhabited, and the Divine in me must operate just as it operates upon the Universal plane. This meant that my whole world of circumstances, friends, and conditions would ultimately become a world of contentment and enjoyment of which "I am the center." This would all happen just as soon as I was able to control my mind and thereby provide a concrete center around which the Divine energies could play.

Surely it was worth trying for. If Troward had found this truth, why not it the idea held me to my task. Later I determined to study with the man who had realized and given to the world so great a statement it had lifted me from my state of despondency.

The immediate difficulty was the need for increased finances.

9

How I Attracted to Myself Twenty Thousand Dollars

IN the laboratory of experience in which my newly revealed relation to the Divine operation was to be tested, the first problem was a financial one. My income was a stipulated one quite enough for my everyday needs, but it did not seem sufficient to enable me to go comfortably to England, where Troward lived and remain for an indefinite period to study with so great a teacher as he must be.

So before inquiring whether Troward took pupils, or whether I would be eligible in case he did, I began to use the paragraph I had memorized. Daily, in fact, almost hourly, the words were in my mind: "My mind is a center of Divine operation, and Divine operation means expansion into something better than has gone before."

From the Edinburgh Lectures I had read something about the Law of Attraction, and from the Chapter on "Causes and Conditions" I had gleaned a vague idea of visualizing. So every night, before going to sleep, I made a mental picture of the desired $20,000 which seemed necessary to go and study with Troward.

Twenty imaginary $1,000 bills were counted over each night in my bedroom, and then, with the idea of more emphatically impressing my mind with the fact that this twenty thousand dollars was for the purpose of going to England and studying with Troward, I wrote out my picture, saw myself buying my steamer ticket, walking up and down the ship's deck from New York to London, and finally, saw myself accepted as Troward's pupil. This process was repeated every morning and every evening, always impressing more and more fully upon my mind Troward's memorized statement: "My mind is a center of Divine operations." I endeavored to keep this statement in the back part of my consciousness all the time, with no thought in mind of how the money might be obtained. Probably the reason why there was no thought of the avenues through which the money might reach me was because I could not possibly imagine where the $20,000 would come from. So I simply held my thought steady and let the power of attraction find its own ways and means.

One day while walking on the street, taking deep breathing exercises, the thought came:

"My mind is surely a center of Divine operation. If God fills all space, then God must be in my mind also; if I want this money to study with Troward that I may know the truth of Life, then both the money and the truth must be mine, though I am unable to feel or see the physical manifestations of either. Still," I declared, "it must be mine."

While these reflections were going on in my mind, there seemed to come up from within me the thought: "I Am all the substance there is. Then, from another channel in my brain the answer seemed to come, "Of course, that's it;

everything must have its beginning in mind. The idea must contain within itself the only one and primary substance there is, and this means money as well as everything else." My mind accepted this idea, and immediately all the tension of mind and body was relaxed.

There was a feeling of absolute certainty of being in touch with all the power Life has to give. All thought of money, teacher, or even my own personality, vanished in the great wave of joy which swept over my entire being. I walked on and on, with this feeling of joy steadily increasing and expanding until everything about me seemed aglow with resplendent light. Every person I passed appeared illuminated as I was. All consciousness of personality had disappeared, and in its place there came that great and almost overwhelming sense of joy and contentment.

That night when I made my picture of the twenty thousand dollars it was with an entirely changed aspect. On previous occasions, when making my mental picture, I had felt that I was waking up something within myself. This time there was no sensation of effort. I simply counted over the twenty thousand dollars. Then, in a most unexpected manner, from a source of which I had no consciousness at the time, there seemed to open a possible avenue through which the money might reach me.

At first it took great effort not to be excited. It all seemed so wonderful, so glorious, to be in touch with supply. But had not Troward cautioned his readers to keep all excitement out of their minds in the first flush of realization of union with Infinite supply, and to treat this fact as a perfectly natural result which had been reached through our demand? This was even more difficult for me than it was to hold the thought that "all the substance there is, I Am; I (idea) Am the beginning of all form, visible or invisible."

Just as soon as there appeared a circumstance which indicated the direction through which the twenty thousand dollars might come, I not only made a supreme effort to regard the indicated direction calmly as the first sprout of the seed I had sown in the absolute, but left no stone unturned to follow up that direction, thereby fulfilling my part. By so doing, one circumstance seemed naturally to lead to another, until, step by step, my desired twenty thousand dollars was secured. To keep my mind poised and free from excitement was my greatest effort.

This first concrete fruition of my study of Mental Science as expounded by Troward's book had come by a careful following of the methods he had outlined. In this connection, therefore I can offer to the reader no better gift than to quote Troward's book, "The Edinburgh Lectures," from which may be derived a complete idea of the line of action I was endeavoring to follow. In the chapter on Causes and Conditions he says:

"To get good results we must properly understand our relation to the great impersonal power we are using. It is intelligent, and we are intelligent, and the two intelligences must co-operate." We must not fly in the face of the law expecting it to do for us what it can only do through us; and we must therefore use our intelligence with the knowledge that it is acting as the instrument of a greater intelligence; and because we have this knowledge we may and should cease from all anxiety as to the final result.

"In actual practice we must first form the ideal conception of our object with the definite intention of impressing it upon the Universal Mind—it is this thought that takes such thought out of the region of mere casual fancies and then affirm that our knowledge of the Law is sufficient reason for a calm expectation of a corresponding result, and that therefore all necessary conditions will come to us in due order. We can then turn to the affairs of our daily life with the calm assurance that the initial conditions are either there already or will soon come into view. If we do not at once see them, let us rest content with the knowledge that the spiritual prototype is already in existence and wait till some circumstance pointing in the desired direction begins to shop itself. It may be a very small circumstance, but it is the direction and not the magnitude which is to be taken into consideration.

As soon as we see it we should regard it as the first sprouting of the seed sown in the Absolute, and do calmly, and without excitement, whatever the circumstances seem to require, and then later on we shall see that this doing will in turn lead to a further circumstance in the same direction, until we find ourselves conducted, step by step, to the accomplishment of our object. In this way the understanding of the great principle of the Law of Supply will, by repeated experiences, deliver us more and more completely out of the region of anxious thought and toilsome labor and bring us into a new world where the useful employment of all our powers, whether mental or physical, will only be an unfolding of our individuality upon the lines of its own nature, and therefore a perpetual source of health and happiness; a sufficient inducement, surely, to the careful study of the laws governing the relation on between the individual and the Universal Mind."

To my mind, then as now, this quotation outlines the core and center of the method and manner of approach necessary for coming in touch with Infinite Supply. At least it, together with the previously quoted statement, "My mind is a center of Divine operation," etc., constituted the only apparent means of attracting to myself the twenty thousand dollars. My constant endeavor to get into the spirit of these statements, and to attract to myself this needed sum, took about six weeks, at the end of which time I had in my bank the required twenty thousand dollars. This could be made into a long story, giving all the details, but the facts, as already narrated, will give you a definite idea of the magnetic condition of my mind while the twenty thousand dollars was finding its way to me.

How I Became The Only Personal Pupil of Thomas Troward, The Great Mental Scientist

AS soon as the idea of studying with Troward came to me, I asked a friend to write him for me, feeling that perhaps my friend could couch my desire in better or more persuasive terms than I could employ. To all the letters written by this friend, I received not one reply. This was so discouraging that I would have completely abandoned the idea of becoming Troward's pupil, except for the experience I had had that day on the street, when my whole world was illuminated, and I remembered the promise "All things whatsoever thou wilt, believe thou hast received, and thou shalt receive."

With this experience in my mind, my passage to England was arranged, notwithstanding the fact that apparently my letters were ignored. We wrote again, however, and finally received a reply, very courteous though very positive. Troward did not take pupils; he had no time to devote to a pupil. Notwithstanding this definite decision, I declined to be discouraged, because of the memory of my experience upon the day when the light and the thought had come to me, "I Am all the Substance there is." I seemed to be able to live that experience over at will, and with it there always came a flood of courage and renewed energy. We journeyed on to London, and from there telegraphed Troward, asking for an interview. The telegram was promptly answered, setting a date when he could see us.

At this time Troward was living in Ruan Manor, a little out-ofthe-way place in the Southern part of England, about twenty miles from a railway station. We could not find it on the map, and with great difficulty Cook's Touring Agency, in London, located the place for us. There was very little speculation in my mind as to what Troward would say to me in this interview. There always remained the feeling that the truth was mine; also that it would grow and expand in my consciousness until peace and contentment were outward, as well as inward, manifestations of my individual life.

We arrived at Troward's house in a terrific rainstorm, and were cordially received by Troward himself, whom I found, much to my surprise, to be more the type of a Frenchman than an Englishman, (I afterward learned that he was a descendant of the Huguenot race), a man of medium stature, with a rather large head, big nose, and eyes that fairly danced with merriment.

After we had been introduced to the other members of the family and given a cup of hot tea, we were invited into the living-room, where Troward talked very freely of everything except my proposed studies. It seemed quite impossible to bring him to that subject. Just before we were leaving, however, I asked quite boldly: "Will you not reconsider your decision to take a personal pupil? I wish so much to study with you," to which he replied, with a very indifferent manner, that he did not feel he could give the time it would require for personal instruction, but that he would be glad to give me the names of two or three books which he felt would not only be interesting but instructive to me.

He said he felt much flattered and pleased that I had come all the way from America to study with him, and as we walked out through the lane from his house to our automobile, his manner became less indifferent, a feeling of sympathy seemed to touch his heart, and he turned to me with the remark: "You might write to me, if so inclined, after you get to Paris, and perhaps, if I have time in the autumn, we could arrange something, though it does not seem possible now."

I lost no time in following up his very kind invitation to write. My letters were all promptly and courteously answered, but there was never a word of encouragement as to my proposed studies. Finally, about two months later, there came a letter with this question in it: "What do you suppose is the meaning of this verse in the 21st Chapter of Revelation?"

"16. And the city lieth foursquare and the length is as large as the breadth; and he measured the city with the reed, twelve thousand furlongs. The length and the breadth and the height of it are equal."

Instinctively I knew that my chance to study with Troward hung upon my giving the correct answer to that question. The definition of the verse seemed utterly beyond my reach. Naturally, answers came to my mind, but I knew intuitively that they were incorrect. I began bombarding my scholarly friends and acquaintances with the same questions. Lawyers, doctors, priests, nuns, and clergymen, all over the world, received letters from me with this question in them. Answers began to return to me, but intuition told me not one was correct.

All the while I was endeavoring to find the answer for myself, but no answer came. I memorized the verse in order that I might meditate upon it. I began a search of Paris for the books Troward had recommended to me, and after two or three days' search we crossed the River Seine to the fle de Cite to go into some of the old bookstores there. The books were out of print, and these were the last places in which to find them. Finally we came upon a little shop which had them. The man had only one copy of each left, consequently the price was high. While remonstrating with the clerk, my eye rested upon the work of an astrologer, which I laughingly picked up and asked: "Do you think Prof.— would read my horoscope?" The clerk looked aghast at the suggestion, and responded, "Why, no, Madame, he is one of France's greatest astrologers. He does not read horoscopes."

In spite of this answer, there was a persistent impulse within me to go to the man. The friend who had accompanied me in my search for the books remonstrated with me, and tried in every way to dissuade me from going to the famous astrologer, but I insisted. When we arrived at his office, I found it somewhat embarrassing to ask him to read my horoscope. Nevertheless, there was nothing to do but put the question. Reluctantly, the Professor invited us into his paper-strewn study; reluctantly, and also impatiently he asked us to be seated. Very courteously and coldly he told me that he did not read horoscopes. His whole manner said, more clearly than words could, that he wished we would take our departure.

My friend stood up. I was at a great loss what to do next, because I felt that I was not quite ready to go. Intuition seemed to tell me there was something for me to gain there. Just what it was I was unable to define, so I paused a moment, much to my friend's displeasure and embarrassment, when one of the Professor's enormous Persian cats jumped into my lap. "Get down, Jack!" the Professor shouted. "What does it mean?" he seemed to ask himself. Then with a greater interest than he had hitherto shown in me, the Professor said with a smile:

"I have never known that cat to go to a stranger before, Madame; my cat pleads for you. I, also, now feel an interest in your horoscope, and if you will give me the data it will give me pleasure to write it out for you."

There was a great feeling of happiness in me when he made this statement, which he concluded by saying, "I do not feel that you really care for your horoscope." The truth of this statement shocked me, because I did not care about a horoscope, and could not give any reason why I was letting him do it. "However," he said, "may I call for your data next Sunday afternoon?"

On Sunday afternoon at the appointed time, the Professor arrived, and I was handing him the slip of paper with all the data of my birth, etc., when the idea came to ask the Professor the answer to the question Troward had given me from the 16th verse of the 21st Chapter of Revelation. The thought was instantly carried into effect, and I found myself asking this man what he thought this verse meant. Without pausing to think it over, he immediately replied, "It means: the city signifies the truth, and the truth is non-invertible; every side from which you approach it is exactly the same." Intuitively and undoubtingly I recognized this answer as the true one, and my joy knew no bounds, because I felt sure that with this correct answer in my possession, Troward would accept me as his pupil in the fall.

As the great astrologer was leaving, I explained to him all about my desire to study with Troward, how I had come from New York City for that express purpose, seemingly to no avail, until the answer to this test question had been given to me by him. He was greatly interested and asked many questions about Troward, and when asked if he would please send me his bill, he smilingly replied, "Let me know if the great Troward accepts you as his pupil," and bade me good afternoon. I hastened to my room to send a telegram to Troward, giving my answer to the question from the 16th verse of the 21st Chapter of Revelation.

There was an immediate response from Troward which said:

"Your answer is correct. Am beginning a course of lectures on The Great Pyramid in London. If you wish to attend them, will be pleased to have you, and afterward, if you still wish to study with me, I think it can be arranged." On receipt of this reply preparations were at once made to leave Paris for London.

I attended all the lectures, receiving much instruction from them, after which arrangements were made for my studying with Troward. Two days before leaving for Cornwall, I received the following letter from Troward clearly indicating the line of study he gave me:

31 Stanwick Road,

W. Kensington, England. Dear Mrs. Behrend:

I think I had better write you a few lines with regard to your proposed studies with me, as I should be sorry for you to be under any misapprehension and so to suffer any disappointment.

I have studied the subject now for several years, and have a general acquaintance with the leading features of most of the systems which, unfortunately, occupy attention in many circles at the present time, such as Theosophy, The Tarot, The Kabala, and the like, and I have no hesitation in saying that, to the best of my judgment, all sorts and descriptions of so-called occult study are in direct opposition to the real life-giving Truth, and therefore, you must not expect any teaching on such lines as these.

We hear a great deal these days about initiation; but, believe me, the more you try to become a so-called "Initiate" the further you will put yourself from living life.

I speak after many years of careful study and consideration when I say that the Bible and its Revelation of Christ is the one thing really worth studying, and that is a subject large enough in all conscience, embracing, as it does, our outward life and of everyday concerns, and also the inner springs of our life and all that we can in general terms conceive of the life in the unseen after putting off the body at death.

You have expressed a very great degree of confidence in my teaching, and if your confidence is such that you wish, as you say, to put yourself entirely under my guidance, I can only accept it as a very serious responsibility, and should have to ask you to exhibit that confidence by refusing to look into such so-called "Mysteries" as I would forbid you to look into. I am speaking from experience; but the result will be that much of my teaching will appear to be very simple, perhaps to some extent dogmatic, and you will say you have heard much of it before.

Faith in God, Prayer and Worship, approach to the Father through Christ—all this is in a certain sense familiar to you; and all I can hope to do is perhaps to throw a little more light on these subjects, that they may become to you, not merely traditional words, but present living facts.

I have been thus explicit as I do not want you to have any disappointment, and also I should say that our so-called course of study will be only friendly conversations at such times as we can fit them in, either you coming to our house, or I to yours, as may be most convenient at the time.

Also, I will lend you some books which will be helpful, but they are very few, and in no sense occult.

Now, if all this falls in with your ideas, we shall, I am sure, be very glad to see you at Ruan Manor, and you will find that the residents there, though few, are very friendly and the neighborhood very pretty.

But, on the other hand, if you feel that you want some other source of learning, do not mind saying so, only you will never find any substitute for Christ.

I trust you will not mind my writing you like this, but I do not want you to come all the way down to Cornwall, and then be disappointed.

With kindest regards,

Yours sincerely,

(Signed)

11

How To Bring The Power In Your Word Into Action

IN every word you use, there is a power germ which expands and projects itself in the direction your word indicates, and ultimately develops into physical expression. For example, you wish the consciousness of joy. Repeat the word "joy" secretly, persistently and emphatically. The repetition of the word joy sets up a quality of vibration which causes the joy germ to begin to expand and project itself until your whole being is filled with joy. This is not a mere fancy, but a truth. Once you experience this power, you will daily prove to yourself that these facts have not been fabricated to fit a theory, but the theory has been built up by careful observation of facts. Everyone knows that joy comes from within. No one can give it to you. Another may give you cause for joy, but no one can be joyous for you. Joy is a state of consciousness, and consciousness is purely mental.

Troward says the "Mental faculties always work under something which stimulates them, and this stimulus may come either from without, through the external senses, or from within, by the consciousness of something not perceptible on the physical plane. The recognition of this interior source of stimulus enables you to bring into your consciousness any state you desire." Once a thing seems normal to you, it is as surely yours, through the Law of growth and attraction, as it is yours to know addition after you have learned the use of figures.

This method of repeating the word makes the word in all of its limitless meaning yours, because words are the embodiment of thoughts, and thought is creative; neither good nor bad, simply creative. This is the reason why Faith builds up and Fear destroys. "Only believe, and all things are possible unto you." It is Faith that gives you dominion over every adverse circumstance or condition. It is your word of Faith that sets you free; not faith in any specific thing or act, but simple Faith in your best self in all ways. It is this ever-present Creative Power within the heart of the word that makes your health, your peace of mind, and your financial condition a reproduction of your most habitual thought.

Try to believe and understand this, and you will find yourself Master of every adverse circumstance or condition, for you will become a Prince of Power.

12

How To Increase Your Faith

BUT you ask, "How can I speak the word of Faith when I have little or no faith?"

Every living thing has faith in something or somebody. Faith is that quality of Power which gives the Creative Energy a corresponding vitality, and the vitality in the word of Faith you use causes it to take corresponding physical form. Even intense fear is alive with faith. You fear smallpox because you believe it possible for you to contract it. You fear poverty and loneliness because you believe them possible for you. It is the Faith which understands that every creation had its birth in the womb of thought-words, that gives you dominion over all things, your lesser self-included, and this feeling of faith is increased and intensified through observing what it does.

Your constant observation should be of your state of consciousness when you did; not when you hoped you might, but feared it was too good to be true. How did you feel that time when you simply had to bring yourself into a better frame of mind and did, or you had to have a certain thing and got it? Live these experiences over again and again—mentally—until you really feel in touch with the self which knows and does, and then the best there is, is yours.

13

The Reward of Increased Faith

YOUR desire to be your best has expanded your faith into the faith of the Universe which knows no failure, and has brought you into conscious realization that you are not a victim of the universe, but a part of it. Consequently you are able to recognize that there is that within yourself which is able to make conscious contact with the Universal Law, and enables you to press all the particular laws of Nature, whether visible or invisible, into serving your particular demand or desire. Thereby you find yourself Master, not a slave, of any situation. Troward tells us that this Mastering is to be "accomplished by knowledge, and the only knowledge which will afford this purpose in all its measureless immensity is the knowledge of the personal element in universal spirit," and its reciprocity to our own personality. In other words, the words you think, the personality you feel yourself to be, are all reproductions in miniature of God, "or specialized universal spirit." All your word-thoughts were God word-forms before they were yours.

The words you use are the instruments—channels—through which the creative energy takes form. Naturally, this sensitive Creative Power can only reproduce in accordance with the instrument through which it passes. All disappointments and failures are the result of endeavoring to think one thing and produce another. This is just as impossible as it would be for an electric fan to be used for lighting purposes, or for water to flow through a crooked pipe in a straight line. The water must take the shape of the pipe through which it flows. Even more truly this sensitive, invisible Substance must reproduce outwardly the shape of the thought-word through which it passes. This is the law of its Nature; therefore, it logically follows, "As a man thinketh, so is he."

Hence, when your thought or word-form is in correspondence with the Eternal constructive and forward movement of the Universal Law, then your mind is the mirror in which the Infinite Power and Intelligence of the Universe sees itself reproduced, and your individual life becomes one of harmony.

14

How to Make Nature Respond to You

IT should be steadily borne in mind that there is an Intelligence and Power in all Nature and all space, which is always creative and infinitely sensitive and responsive. The responsiveness of its nature is two-fold: it is creative, and amenable to suggestion. Once the human understanding grasps this all-important fact, it realizes the simplicity with which the law of life supplies your every demand.

All that is necessary is to realize that your mind is a center of Divine operation, and consequently contains that within itself which accepts suggestions, and expect all life to respond to your call. Then you will find suggestions which tend to the fulfillment of your desire coming to you, not only from your fellowmen, but also from the flowers, the grass, the trees, and the rocks, which will enable you to fulfill your heart's desire, if you act upon them in confidence on this physical plane.

"Faith without works is dead," but Faith with Works sets you absolutely free.

15

Faith with Works – What It has Accomplished

IT is said of Tyson, the great Australian Millionaire, that the suggestion to "make the desert land of Australia blossom as the rose" came to him from a modest little Australian violet while he was working as a bushman for something like three shillings a day.

He used to find these friendly little violets growing in certain places in the woods, and something in the flower touched something akin to itself in the mind of Tyson. He would sit on the side of his bunk at night and wonder how flowers and vegetable life could be given an opportunity to express themselves in the desert land of Australia. No doubt he realized that it would take a long time to save enough money to put irrigating ditches in the desert lands, but his thought and feeling assured him it could be accomplished, and if it could be done, he could do it.

If there was a power within himself which was able to capture the idea, then there must be a responsive power within the idea itself which could bring itself into a practical physical manifestation. He resolutely put aside all questions as to the specific ways and means which would be employed in bringing his desire into physical manifestation, and simply kept his thought centered upon the idea of making fences and seeing flowers and grass where none existed at that time.

Since the responsiveness of Reproductive Creative Power is not limited to any local condition of mind, his habitual meditation and mental picture set his ideas free to roam in infinitude, and attract to themselves other ideas of a kindred nature. Therefore, it was not necessary for Tyson to wait until he had saved from his three shillings a day enough money to irrigate the land, to see his ideas and desires fulfilled, for his ideas found other ideas in the financial world which were attuned in sympathy with themselves, and doors of finance were quickly opened.

All charitable institutions are maintained upon the principle of the responsiveness of life. If this were not true, no one would care to give, simply because another needed. The law of demand and supply, cause and effect, can never be broken. Ideas attract to themselves kindred ideas. Sometimes they come from a flower, a book, or out of the invisible. You are intent upon an idea not quite complete as to the ways and means of fulfillment, and behold along comes another idea, from no one can tell where, and find friendly lodging with your idea; one idea attracting another, and so on until your desires are physical facts.

You may feel the necessity for improvement in your finances, and wonder how this increase is to be brought about, when there seems suddenly to come from within the idea itself, the realization that everything—even money—had its birth in thought, and your thoughts turn their course. You simply hold to the statement or affirmation that the best, and all there is, is yours. Since you are able to capture ideas from the Infinite through the instrument of your intuition, you let your mind rest upon that thought, knowing full well that this very thought will respond to itself. Your inhibition of all doubt and anxiety enables the reassuring ideas to establish themselves and attract to them "I can" and "I will" ideas, which gradually grow into the physical form of the desire in your mind.

In the conscious uses of the Universal Power to reproduce your desires in physical form, three facts should be borne in mind:

First—All space is filled with a Creative Power.

Second—This Creative Power is amenable to suggestion.

Third—It can only work by deductive methods.

As Troward tells us, this last is an exceedingly important point, for it implies that the action of the ever-present Creative Power is in no way limited by precedent. It works according to the essence of the spirit of the principle. In other words, this Universal Power takes its creative direction from the word you give it. Once man realizes this great truth, the character with which this sensitive, reproductive power is invested becomes the most important of all his considerations. It is the unvarying law of Creative Life Principle that "As a man thinketh in his heart, so is he." If you realize the truth that the Creafive Power can be to you only what you feel and think it to be, it is willing and able to meet your demands.

Troward says, "If you think your thought is Powerful, your
Thought is Powerful."

"As a man thinketh in his heart, so is he" is the law of life, and the Creative Power can no more change this law than an ordinary mirror can reflect back to you a different image than the object you hold before it. "As you think, so are you" does not mean "as you tell people you think," or "as you would wish the world to believe you think." It means your innermost thoughts; that place where no one but you know. "None can know the Father save the son," and "No one can know the son but the Father."

Only the reproductive Creative Spirit of Life knows what you think until your thoughts become physical facts and manifest themselves in your body, your brain, or your affairs. Then everyone with whom you come into contact may know, because the Father, the Intelligent Creative Energy which heareth in secret your most secret thoughts, rewards you openly reproduces your thoughts in physical form. "As you think, that is what you become" should be kept in the background of your mind constantly. This is watching and praying without ceasing, and when you are not feeling quite up to par physically, pray.

16

Suggestions as to How to Pray or Ask, believing you have already received.

Scientific Thinking – Positive Thought. Suggestions for Practical Application

Try, through careful, positive, enthusiastic (though not strenuous) thought, to realize that the indescribable, Invisible Substance of Life fills all space; that its nature is Intelligent, Undifferentiated Substance.

Five o'clock in the morning is the best time to go into this sort of meditation.

If you will retire early every night for one month, and before falling asleep, impress firmly upon your subjective mind the affirmation: "My Father is the ruler of all the world, and is expressing His directing power through me," you will find that the substance of life takes form in your thought molds. Do not accept the above suggestion simply because it is given to you. Think it over carefully until the impression is made upon your own subconscious mind understandingly.

Rise every morning, as was suggested before, at five o'clock, sit in a quiet room in a straight-back chair, and think out the affirmation of the previous evening, and you will realize and be able to put into practice your Princely Power with the realization to some extent, at least, that your mind really is a center through which all the Creative Energy and Power there is, is taking form.

Scientific Prayer
The Principle Underlying Scientific Prayer

In prayer for a change in condition, physical, mental, or financial, for yourself or another, bear in mind that the fundamental necessity for the answer to prayer is the understanding of the scientific statement:

"Ask, believing you have already received, And you shall receive"

This is not as difficult as it appears on the surface, once you realize that:

Everything has, its origin in the mind, and that which you seek outwardly, you already possess.

No one can think a thought in the future.

Your thought of a thing constitutes its origin.

THEREFORE:

The Thought Form of the Thing is already Yours As
soon as you think it.

Your steady recognition of this Thought Possession causes the thought to concentrate, to condense, to project itself, and to assume physical form.

To Get Rich Through Creation

The recognition or conception of new sources of wealth is the loftiest aspiration you can take into your heart, for it assumes and implies the furtherance of all noble aims.

Items to be remembered about Prayer for Yourself or Another

(Remember that that which you call treatment or prayer is not, in any sense, hypnosis. It should never be your endeavor to take possession of the mind of another.)

Remember that it should never be your intention to make yourself believe that which you know to be untrue. You are simply thinking into God or First Cause with the understanding that:

"If a thing is true at all, there is a way in which it is true throughout the universe." Remember that the power of thought works by absolutely scientific principles. These principles are expressed in the language of the statement:

"As a man thinketh in his heart, so is he." This statement contains a world of wisdom, but man's steady recognition and careful application of the statement itself is required to bring it into practical use.

Remember that the principles involved in being as we think in our heart are elucidated and revealed by the law: "As you sow, so shall you reap". Remember that your freedom to choose just what you will think, just what thought possession you will affirm and claim, constitutes God's gift to you.

It shows how First Cause has endowed every man with the power and ability to bring into his personal environment whatever he chooses.

Cause and Effect in reference to Getting

If you plant an ACORN, you get an OAK.

If you sow a GRAIN OF CORN, you reap a stalk and MANY kernels of corn.

You always get the manifestation of that which you consciously or unconsciously AFFIRM and CLAIM, habitually declare and expect, or, in other words, "AS YOU SOW."

Therefore, sow the seeds of—

I AM. . .I OUGHT TO DO. . .I CAN DO... I WILL DO.

Realize

—that because you ARE you OUGHT to do; —that because you OUGHT to, you CAN do; —that because you CAN do, you DO do.

The manifestation of this truth, even in a small degree, gives you the undisputable understanding that DOMINION IS YOUR CHARTER RIGHT.

You are an heir of First Cause, endowed with all the power He has.

God has given you everything. ALL is yours, and you know that all you have to do is to reach out your mental hand and take it.

This Formula may serve as a pattern to shape your own Prayer or Affirmation into God for the benefit of another or yourself.

If for another, you speak the Christian name of the person you wish to help; then dismiss their personality entirely from your consciousness.

Intensify your thought by meditating upon the fact that there is that in you which finds the way, which is the Truth and is the Life.

You are affirming this fact, believing that since you are thinking this, it is already yours. Having lifted up your feeling to the central idea of this meditation, you examine your own consciousness and see if there is aught which is unlike God. If there is any feeling of fear, worry, malice, envy, hatred, or jealousy turn back in your meditation to cleanse your thought through the affirmation that God's love and purity fills all space, including your heart and soul. Reconcile your thought with the love of God, always remembering that:

You are made in the Image and Likeness of Love.

Keep this cleansing thought in mind until you feel that you have freed your consciousness entirely of all thoughts and feelings other than: Love and Unity with all Humanity.

Then if denials do not disturb you, deny all that is unlike your desired manifestation. This accomplished, you almost overlay your denial with the affirmative thought that You are made in the Image and Likeness of God, and already have your desire fulfilled in its first, its original thought-form.

Closing of prayer

Prayer as a method of thought is a deliberate use of the Law which gives you the power of dominion over everything which tends in any way to hamper your perfect liberty.

YOU HAVE BEEN GIVEN LIFE
THAT YOU MAY ENJOY IT MORE AND MORE
FULLY.

The steady recognition of this Truth makes you declare yourself a PRINCE OF POWER.

You recognize, accept, and use this power as THE CHILD OF A KING, AND HENCE DOMINION IS YOUR BIRTHRIGHT.

Then when you feel the light of this great truth flooding your consciousness—open the flood-gates of your soul in heartfelt praise because you have the understanding that THE CREATOR AND HIS CREATION ARE ONE; also that the Creator is continually creating through his creation.

Close your treatment in the happy assurance that the prayer which is fulfilled is not a form of supplication, but a steady habitual affirming that: "The Creator of all creation is operating specifically through me," therefore—

THE WORK MUST BE PERFECTLY DONE.

YOUR MIND IS A CENTER OF DIVINE OPERATION

Hints for application and Practice

For every five minutes given to reading and study of the theories of Mental Science, spend fifteen minutes in the use and application of the knowledge acquired.

1. Spend one minute in every twenty-four hours to conscientiously thinking over the specification that must be observed in order to have your prayers answered.

2. Practice the steady recognition of desirable thought possession for two periods of fifteen minutes each every day. Not only time yourself each period to see how long you can keep a given conception before your mental vision, but also keep a written record of the vividness with which you experience your mental image. Remember that your mental senses are just as varied and trainable as your physical ones.

3. Spend five minutes every day between 12 noon and 1 o'clock with a mental research for new sources of wealth.

17

Things to Remember

THAT the greatest Mental Scientist the world has ever known (Jesus Christ, the Man) said all things are possible unto you.

Also, "the things I do, you can do." Did he tell the truth?

Jesus did not claim to be more divine than you are. He declared the whole human race children of God. By birth he was no exception to this rule. The power He possessed was developed through His personal effort. He said you could do the same if you would only believe in yourself.

A great idea is valueless unless accompanied by physical action. God gives the idea; man works it out upon the physical plane.

All that is really worthwhile is contentment. Self-command alone can produce it.

The soul and body are one. Contentment of mind is contentment of soul, and contentment of soul means contentment of body.

If you wish health, watch your thoughts, not only of your physical being, but your thoughts about everything and everybody. With your will, keep them in line with your desire, and outwardly act in accordance with your thoughts, and you will soon realize that all power both over thoughts and conditions has been given to you.

You believe in God. Believe in yourself as the physical instrument through which God operates.

Absolute dominion is yours when you have sufficient self-mastery to conquer the negative tendency of thoughts and actions.

Ask yourself daily: "What is the purpose of the Power which put me here?"

"How can I work with the purpose for life and liberty in me?" After having decided these questions, endeavor hourly to fulfill them. You are a law unto yourself.

If you have a tendency to overdo anything: eat, drink, or blame circumstances for your misfortunes, conquer that tendency with the inward conviction that all power is yours. Eat less, drink less, blame circumstances less, and the best there is will gradually grow in the place where the worst seemed to be.

Always remember that all is yours to use as you will. You can if you will; if you will, you do.

God the Father blesses you with all He has to give. Make good Godly use of it. The reason for greater success when you first began your studies and demonstrations in Mental Science was your joy and enthusiasm at the simple discovery of Power within, which was greater than you were able to put into your understanding later. With increased understanding comes increasing joy and enthusiasm, and the results will correspond.

THE END

BOOK THREE
HOW TO LIVE LIFE AND LOVE IT

Genevieve Behrend

Foreword

The purpose of this series of personal-pointer Lessons, which are herein compiled into one volume, is to indicate in a clear, concise way "the natural principles governing the relation between the creative action of all thought-power and material things," i.e., circumstances and conditions.

If these few simple principles are carefully studied, and mastered to your satisfaction, and then put into practical, hourly application, the student will find very soon that it is possible for man to make conscious contact with the Almighty, Ever-Present, Never-Failing God; and this just naturally means individual FREEDOM, freedom from every form of limitation and bondage of any nature. (Read Mark 9:23.) Then try to believe that the Spirit of Life, which is your life also, knows "How to Live Life and Love It."

All the joy Life has to give is yours right now! Let us start on the highway to unqualified success now. God is our guide.

Your loving companion,

-- Genevieve Behrend

1

Live Life And Love It!

MASTER: Let us begin this morning's lesson with the certain knowledge that every living thing really wishes to enjoy Life. Once one really has entered into the true Spirit of Life that one can not help loving to live and is certain to enjoy life.

PUPIL: That is just it. If one could get into the Spirit of Living Life, I am sure one, every one, would enjoy it. But it seems to me that the general run of humanity live in the spirit of death rather than of life. The average person I know is always wishing that he could but at the same time knowing that he can't. That does not seem like really living.

MASTER: Indeed that is not living and people who live in that form of mental action are "the living dead." Let us see if we cannot find an easy, logical method of entering into the true Spirit of Life. We know that we must enter into the Spirit of a book, or a picture, or of music, else they are entirely meaningless to us. To really appreciate anything we must share the mental attitude of the creative thought and feeling which brought them into outward form.

PUPIL: Now I am wondering if getting into the spirit of a thing would be getting into the spiritual prototype of the thing we may wish to enjoy. For example, I should very much enjoy a home of my own, a husband and children. Can one really get into the spirit of these good things before one does have them, or before one can see them in form?

MASTER: I am pleased that you mention the spiritual prototype is the spiritual, or mental, purpose of a thing, and is the true place of origin of anything. So you wish a home, husband, children?

PUPIL: Yes, a home in the country, not a large house, one just large enough that we can live in every room of it.

MASTER: The house is to be the home?

PUPIL: Why yes, of course.

MASTER: I asked this, you see, because just a house may not always be a home while a mere tent may be. Your prototype for the home would be PROTECTION, SHELTER, FREEDOM. To begin at the beginning let us get into the FEELING of perfect protection, shelter, freedom. Let us really feel in tune with these qualities of Spirit; and they in their turn will attract unto us the ways and means for the home.

PUPIL: So far I have been jumbling everything together in my thought. Should I not take each thing separately and try to enter into the spiritual origin, or purpose, of that one thing before going on to another?

MASTER: By all means finish planting one thought securely in the mind before trying to introduce another. After you have really tuned into the feeling of PROTECTION, SHELTER, SECURITY, FREEDOM, then begin to mentally build your house and people it with a husband and children. Thus you are making a mental picture of the forms you wish the Creative Energy to take. Be specific and accurate in making your mental picture, remembering that the mental picture you make is the mould into which the unformed Spirit is poured for solidifying into actual, outward form. The house itself may be a bungalow, or a two-story house, or may be of brick, or stone, or wood, or what not. It may have any number of rooms, doors, windows, a fire-place, etc. In other words you must first mentally blueprint your house. When your mental picture is perfectly finished, and your FEELING is that these things ARE yours NOW, and you KNOW that your mind is in perfect tune with the Source of all things, then, and not until then, are you ready to take the next step into the attainment of your desires.

PUPIL: But the matter of the right husband, that seems very difficult for me. First, I am not in the right position to contact men and now I have only two men acquaintances, neither of which I should care to live with in my model home.

MASTER: What you say does not enter into the matter at all. All that the individual does is to place into the Originating Creative Power the QUALITY one wishes to differentiate, just as one plugs into the electric current in the house when one wishes to use it. The light, the heater, the Frigidaire, the fan, the iron, or any other thing one may want to use, all are there. All of the power is already there, too. It is ready and waiting; all that is necessary is your RECOGNITION of it and your taking action to utilize it. Your recognition and your desire cause you to make the right contact; and the power that is there does all the rest. The ways and means of your meeting the one and only husband are not your own concern; they form themselves into line automatically as a result of your turning on the correct switch.

PUPIL: Do you mean that it is not necessary for me to do anything to try to meet people? Do I not have to go to parties, or visit friends? Sometimes when I should be much happier at home I go to such places, and do such things, because there is always a chance of meeting the right one there.

MASTER: All of that is entirely unnecessary. The power you have turned on within yourself is an ATTRACTING Power, remember! To give you an example: One time when we were in Chicago, living at the Medinah Athletic Club, a young lady came to me with much the same attitude that you express and received the same answer I give here. She was a trained nurse, a graduate of St. Luke's. She was tired of living alone, wished a home, a husband, children. After she had had ten or twelve personal interviews and lessons with me I told her, one morning as she was leaving our apartment, that it would not be necessary for her to come to see me again. She felt sure also that the contact had been made. Our apartment was on the forty-second floor; and as she caught the elevator down she said a "great wave of peace and contentment came over her."

In her heart she had the consciousness of love and protection even now. At the thirty-fourth floor the elevator stopped and a young man who was very ill got into the elevator. Almost at once he folded up on the floor, unconscious. The elevator operator knew him since he had an apartment in the building; and the nurse and operator together got the man back to his apartment, into bed, and sent for the house physician who said that the nurse had done exactly the right thing. In about an hour the man regained consciousness and sent for his own physician who wished to assign a nurse of his own choosing to the case. But the patient insisted on having the nurse who had helped him from the elevator, and kept her in attendance on him until he was fully recovered. Just about six months later patient and nurse were married.

PUPIL: That was certainly a lucky break for her, that she should take just that elevator, at that time. That seems to me like drawing the lucky number on bank-night at the theatre. Of course someone always wins but there is no certainty about it, is there?

MASTER: Really the two positions are not at all parallel; they are not even similar. With the nurse it was not luck at all. Deliberately, consciously, in faith, she had plugged into a circuit of great power within herself, the circuit of Universal Power that we call God, or Life and which did produce a perfect reciprocity of feeling and a certain sense of security, protection, provision, companionship. In other words she deliberately "initiated a train of causation directed to her individual purpose," to quote Troward, just as you would attach the cord to your electric-iron if you wished to press clothes. There was no luck in the matter whatsoever; it was purest science manifesting, as it always will and does, in answer to a strong desire scientifically placed. Whether it is plugging in to a circuit of electric energy or tuning in with the Creative Life Principle the procedure is exactly the same.

PUPIL: I am beginning to see the light. But the case you have just told me about still seems rather spectacular and unusual.

MASTER: That is because you have not trained the objective quality of your mind to know that it can always TRUST the Intelligent Creative Spirit of Life within yourself. You are letting preconceived ideas, and shallow and false ones, take precedent in your mind over pure, scientific Principle. You do not feel that you need to know the principles of electricity before you can use your vacuum-cleaner. All we know about electricity is gleaned from what we see it DO. The same thing applies to Life. The innermost principles of Life will always remain a profound mystery. But one can, and should, live life to the full in the self and love it.

PUPIL: I am wondering if the nurse "lived happily ever after" with her unusually-acquired husband. And did they have the home and the children she so much desired?

MASTER: The couple have lived very happily together for a number of years now and do have a comfortable home and three children. I shall explain more of that later. The secret of living life and loving this: First, your feeling towards the livingness of life in you, as well as in all life everywhere, should be to RECOGNIZE Life as Intelligent and to know that when this Intelligence is working through you it does not change its essential nature. It has always been a RECEPTIVE Power, that is AMENABLE TO SUGGESTION, and it is always RESPONSIVE and CREATIVE. This is the basis of Troward's meaning in his words which I use for my own favorite affirmation, and which, quoted, is this:

"My mind IS a center of DIVINE operation. The divine operation is ALWAYS for EXPANSION and fuller EXPRESSION; and this means the production of something beyond what has gone before, something entirely NEW, not included in past experience though proceeding out of it by an orderly sequence of growth. Therefore since the Divine can not change its inherent nature it must operate in the same manner in me; consequently in my own special world, of which I am the center, it will move forward to produce NEW conditions, always in advance of any that have gone before."

Once you really plug your individual consciousness into the great power of the Universe the above will be your line of thinking. You will involuntarily look to the Life-Principle in you, not only as the only Creative Energy but also as a directive Power. That is you will let God determine, through your conscious mind, the actual forms and courses which the conditions for its manifestations will always take in your own individual world. Do remember always that the Originating Spirit of Life (of YOUR life, too) is forever a FORMING Power. It is for this reason that we should use such great care in the selection of our HABITUAL thoughts and feelings -for create they will, and always.

PUPIL: How may I know, for example, that my true husband is being guided to me, or I to him?

MASTER: By your feeling of CERTAINTY, even though outward conditions show no sign of the fact. Still you are SURE. You feel close. You KNOW you are protected. You feel the influence of love all about you. You have stimulated these special qualities of Life in your individual world by your having persistently looked to God, knowing that He does manifest in you. Your mental attitude of faith and trust and expectancy has attracted all the joys of life. You realize that all that Life has to give is present with you NOW just as all that light has to give is present wherever light is.

PUPIL: Do I understand that if I live as closely as possible in the consciousness of reciprocity of feeling, and know that love is guiding, protecting and providing for me with its abundance, I can attract these qualities of life in the form of a man?

MASTER: Yes. For the house and the home FEEL protection, shelter, perfect harmony. For the husband FEEL love and joy; then LIVE IN THE FEELING OF THESE THINGS. Feeling is one of the strongest elements in Life and is also the most responsive.

2

The Fine Art Of Giving

PUPIL: It seems to me that the pace you are setting here is going to be rather severe discipline for me. But since it is to be for only a few weeks, if I wish, I shall try it. If there is not a big change for the better, both inside and out, at the end of that time, I can stop. N'est-ce pas?

MASTER: Yes, but please do not enter lightly upon this study. And do not seek to cultivate an acquaintance with God for the sake of what you will be able to get from Him. This is a tragic mistake that many people make, and which is difficult for many of them to rectify. They seek first to get, and promise faithfully that they will then give. But in so doing they have inverted the Spirit's Law of Compensation, which is good, which is as just as it is good, and which is as immutable as it is both good and just.

PUPIL: This sounds interesting. What is this Great Law?

MASTER: The LAW is that FIRST we must GIVE! And after we have given the getting automatically follows, just as day naturally comes with the rising of the sun. But the getting of anything good never precedes the giving of something of value! TRUE GIVING, giving with love as unto God Himself, cannot possibly impoverish anyone; nor can withholding from the Spirit and its service ever truly enrich one. Verily, " 'tis more blessed to give than to receive!" GIVING as unto God opens wide the Sanctuary of Jehovah within us in which we may always find PEACE. GIVING makes of the giver a direct channel for the transmission of Infinite Love and Power into one's daily, hourly life. Then will adversity flee; and certain achievement of "all things whatsoever ye will" follows immediately. But, I repeat, FIRST ye must GIVE!

PUPIL: But what can we give to God if He already has everything?

MASTER: We can give Him the one thing of which He does not have too much, of which He can never have too much, of which we can never hope to give Him too much. The one thing that God wishes us to give Him, first, last and always, is nothing less than the greatest gift in the Universe. Now what is it?

PUPIL: I am sure that it is Love.

MASTER: Right, but just what is Love?

PUPIL: Why God is Love.

MASTER: That is correct, too. But if God is Love, what is God? And if Love is God, what is Love?

PUPIL: Is this a parable? What is Love? What is God? That's just what I would like to know, too. Tell us please!

MASTER: Just what God is, just what Love is, each person must answer for himself. For after all your own conception of God and of Love IS God and IS Love to you! But perhaps we can set forth a few thoughts that may prove helpful, and which will be practical. To some Love is passion, and can only be conferred upon, or come from, the opposite sex. To some Love is the tenderness of a mother for her child, or of a doting father for his brood. To others Love is the love of friends, parents, or orphans. And there are some who love themselves most of all. But REAL LOVE is Love of God, and for God! To LOVE HIM is the FIRST Commandment! And if one keeps this great commandment there is no need of any other commandment; for if we really DO LOVE GOD, which is the first and greatest of the commandments, we automatically keep inviolate all the others!

PUPIL: But is it enough to just love God with all of our hearts, all of our souls, and all of our minds? Must we not DO something about it as well?

MASTER: Certainly we must do something about it. Love without the fruits of Love is dead! If we love God, we will serve Him devotedly, faithfully, happily, continuously.

PUPIL: How best may we serve Him?

MASTER: BY GIVING OF OURSELVES to our fellowman! By giving of ourselves to our neighbors as unto ourselves. A scientist, one like Doctor Walter Reed for example, who gives his very life, and lovingly and gladly, in order to benefit mankind knows the true love of God. So does the heroic nurse who ministers to afflicted mankind out of sheer love of mankind. So does the self-effacing, self-sacrificing mother, or father, or teacher, or minister. There are many ways in which one may serve. All do not possess scientific talents, nor healing talents, nor comforting talents. But all do possess something they can give! Some who feel themselves unable to serve directly give of themselves by donating money to worthy causes, and these, too, are serving God because they Love their neighbors and therefore Love Him. Let me give you an example of TRUE LOVE as I personally knew it in a wonderful woman, one of many cases that I know.

PUPIL: Yes, do give us an example. They always help to clarify things, and show us how others have done what we wish to do.

MASTER: Very well. This divine soul was reared in a home of great wealth and culture. But as a very young woman she made up her mind to go out into the world, "on the firing-line" itself, as she called it, to serve actively lovingly, there. She became a nun, and as such was assigned to a hospital as a trained nurse. As she entered upon her life-work she was filled with love for mankind, with enthusiasm for serving God by serving his suffering ones. And she did serve lovingly, happily, faithfully, tenderly eight hours a day, or even twelve hours daily. But the hospital was woefully understaffed; and Marie, as we shall call her here, was soon subject to call sixteen hours daily; and even during the eight hours when she was supposed to have her rest she was often summoned and asked to serve more. Her quarters were right on the same floor with many of the patients, and this ward was her charge day and night. Often at two or three o'clock in the morning the bell beside her bed would ring with an urgent summons. She would arise at once, go to the patient and minister to his or her wants. But in due time she became physically tired, and of course she began to resent the calls that broke into her rest, especially when it seemed to her, as it often did at these times, that the patient merely wished a drink of water, or wanted a pillow adjusted a certain way, or was merely lonely, all of which were irritating trifles to a weary nurse.

For a month or more these trials went on, seemingly from bad to worse. Marie resolved almost desperately to do something about it, and immediately. So she cast about for a way to best remedy the situation. For days she thought about the matter, asking the Spirit for guidance. At length the flash came, directly from the Infinite! She took up a little card, wrote down the new motto that had been given her, and fastened it on the wall above her bed, right by the service bell, so that she might see it and be again reminded every time the buzzer rang. On the card she had written: "THE MASTER CALLS!" Of course her system worked from the beginning. Quite soon she was saying in immediate answer to the bell, even while sleepily fumbling for her light: "THE MASTER CALLS!" And she would arise and go and serve, without impatience, without resentment, yes, rejoicing in the opportunity to again serve in love. As a consequence her energy was untiring; she easily and joyfully did the work of three nurses, always rested, always fresh, always efficient, always smiling, whenever called. Her patients loved her greatly. She was always cheerful, always encouraging, always aglow, as it were, with a holy Love. And to those who did not know her secret, as very few did, the patients she attended seemed to be "miraculously healed." Let your motto also be: "THE MASTER CALLS!" And remember that the humblest service that you can render to the lowliest of your fellowmen, if rendered in LOVE, is a direct service to Him!

PUPIL: This is a profoundly beautiful and powerful illustration. Is that the motto, or the principle, that you use in helping the many who come to you? If not, what is your own personal secret of serving?

MASTER: My own method, in a way, is very similar to that of Marie. Like her I wished to serve lovingly, to serve as many as possible, to help to the limit of my powers in alleviating any and all kinds of suffering, physical, mental, spiritual or other form of unhappiness. Not only do I strive always to help those who seek me out. Every person whose hand I take into mine in greeting, every person into whose eyes I look, in all places at all times, yes even the shop girl who sells me my hose, the milkman who comes to my door, the beggar on the street, everyone to whom I speak at any and all times receives the same strong spiritual impulse from me! I INTENTIONALLY SEE THE RADIANT CHRIST IN ALL!

PUPIL: But I thought that you told me once you never mentally treat people unless they ask for help.

MASTER: I don't, not specifically, not specifically under any other circumstances. My secret is this: I have deliberately formed the HABIT of beholding the Christ in every soul that my eyes fall upon! I do not ever see anyone as being poor, or old, or ill, or bereaved, or lonely, or homely, or evil or imperfect in any way. I BEHOLD EACH AND ALL AS ONLY PERFECT! I SEE ONLY THE RADIANT CHRIST in every one of them BECAUSE THE CHRIST IS in each of them!

3

The Art Of Reciprocity

MASTER: The Bible, the sages of all time, all sources of real TRUTH, unite in absolute agreement concerning one great thing, namely: That God and Man are ONE and not two, that the "two" are not separated but indissolubly joined in perfect and harmonious UNION. The Invisible (Spirit) and the visible (form, or matter) actually ARE inseverably connected. Each is a complement of the other. And the whole of Truth is to be found ONLY in the combination of the "two," which really are not "two" but ONE through ETERNAL UNION!

PUPIL: I am particularly happy about this conclusion because I used to think that a person could not have both spiritual and physical blessings at one and the same time. I thought that the physical world had nothing of God in it. Yes, I thought that Spirit was utterly separated from form, or matter. Now I feel sure that the reason I did not make any real progress then was that I was trying to have an inside for Life without an outside, and an outside without any inside. In other words I was simply living in the physical world without being conscious of the fact that forever I have a direct connection with the Spiritual Realm. I am right, am I not, in believing and feeling that I must have the REALIZATION that each is vitally necessary to the other for the formation of a Substantial Entity.

MASTER: Yes, you are exactly right! No one can go very far on the great highway of Truth until he realizes that there never was, and never will be, an inside to anything without an outside also. While one is visible and the other invisible (to the human eye) the ONLY REALITY is in the combination of the two. A constant awareness of this fact on our part brings us that radiant realization of ONE-ness, of UNION, that we must have if we hope to make any progress in Truth.

PUPIL: After this one basic realization what other truths must we have?

MASTER: We must KNOW that underlying the totality of all things is the SOURCE OF ALL THINGS, the Great Cosmic Intelligence. We must know that no physical thing of itself only can ever create anything. The physical form is the INSTRUMENT that Life (God) fashioned of His own Essence in order to have something through which He could work His wonders, and give them form also. But He always LIVES in that instrument! Do not ever lose sight of this fact: The power is always greater than the form through which it manifests, just as electricity is infinitely greater than the bulb through which it manifests as light. It is through UNION of forms, positive with negative, or masculine with feminine, or Spirit with Soul, that the creation of all forms, or channels, or physical things, results. This eternal principle runs all through the Bible, is the warp and woof of it, the whole substance of it. Seek ye the answer in that Great Book!

PUPIL: But many people say that the Bible is "antiquated," that it is a "book of fables," and of "old wives' tales," etc.

MASTER: How does this concern YOU? Which is the more reliable guide, do you think, the spiritually darkened ones who criticised the Bible or thine own soul which knows light when it sees it? Are you going to do your own thinking or shall you be content to let others do it for you, and wrongly? If we must go to other people in our quest of Truth, let us resolve to go to ones who have the light of the Spirit. For instance, what does Troward say of the Bible? Let his Wisdom be our guide here. He tells us that "the Bible is the Book of the EMANCIPATION OF MAN!" He adds that this means man's COMPLETE "DELIVERANCE from sorrow, sickness, poverty, struggle, uncertainty, from ignorance and limitation, and finally from death itself." This noble conception of Troward's is exactly what the Bible IS. With such a wonderful Book in print one should not be surprised to learn that it has the widest circulation of any book ever published, that it is still the world's best seller. If the Bible were not Truth, it would not live through so many generations and still hold its pre-eminent position. So let us proceed on the assumption that Troward is right, that the Bible DOES contain the secret whereby the art of living a perfectly free and happy life may be attained.

PUPIL: But the Bible has never been a very interesting book to me. I have thought of it as "old world fables."

MASTER: It was uninteresting to you because you did not understand it. Nevertheless it is a most scientific Book, full of interesting facts and life-giving Truth, the finest book ever written about the greatest of all the sciences, the Science of LIFE.

PUPIL: My parents were religious people, church every Sunday morning, prayers every day, and all of that. But I could never see that they were any better off, or any happier -if as happy -than the neighbors who never went to church. But I shall be glad to make an honest effort to understand and follow whatever you outline, even the Bible if you say so.

MASTER: I have spoken. And because you are honest in your desire you will be honest in your thinking; and honest thinking makes a true student. Because you truly wish to understand the art of living you shall come to know it, and when you know Life and really live it you are certain to love it. The Bible IS, I repeat the BOOK OF LIFE, and of Life's immutable Laws. Remember always that Life's Laws contain within themselves the solution to EVERY human problem! Indeed "Wisdom is the beginning of magic." The Spirit of Christ, or Intelligent Life, within us is the LIGHT of each of us. It will always make the path easy, interesting and joyous IF only we will study and understand how to use our own Divine Power, and THEN REALLY USE IT. Once one has formed the habit of looking to the Bible for the answer to all problems it becomes to that one as a lantern carried on a dark night. The next steps ahead may be in total darkness, but when you approach the light you carry illuminates the path and you know exactly where to step, and just what to do. Your feeling is influenced in the right direction.

It is true that the Bible veils its most profound secrets in symbols and parables; but the Wisdom is there for the earnest and consecrated seeker! Maybe, the author, was right when he wrote: "The true artist finds that the materials for his art are ever present. But the ones who can discern the possible uses of these varied materials, and who possess the instinct, intuition and training to put them to their best uses are always few in number. The materials out of which art is made are ever present; but THE ARTIST appears only at intervals!" So it is with the mysterious force we call Life. Every person has it; but the ones who understand and use Life's finest possibilities, and who get out of it, consequently, its very richest growth are really very few in number. So let us put into this study of Life our very noblest personal energy.

PUPIL: It seems to me, judging from what you say here and from what you have already taught us in these lessons, that our perfecting of the art of living and loving it is based upon the training of the mind and feeling to the point where we shall find as much joy and satisfaction in self-discipline as we formerly found in self-indulgences. Am I right?

MASTER: Yes. Once one has gone that far on the path, he is then around the last turn and on the "way that is straight," the path of splendor that leads directly to conscious UNION WITH THE FATHER! The Bible says the art of really LIVING and loving Life centers around the record of man's thoughts and feelings, his aspirations, inspirations and experiences, on his discovery of the Life-Spirit as "an ever present help in trouble." When a man has found his REAL SELF (the God-Self, or Christ-Radiance) within, when he has discovered the infinite possibilities and potentialities with which he is forever surrounded, when he LIVES these things and loves the life he lives he becomes the TRUE ARTIST! Then will he use the RIGHT MATERIALS, then will he PRODUCE the RESULTS DESIRED in the form of the picture that he originally conceived!

PUPIL: Suppose one has never had the advantages of higher education, that one's whole life has been commonplace and restricted, would such a one be able to understand and apply these beautiful and interesting truths?

MASTER: Yes indeed! One's station in life does not make the slightest difference.

One may be a woman who is trying to cook a good meal in the one and only room that she has, on a one-burner gas-stove. One may be a man who is a shoe-salesman, and who spends his whole time every day trying to satisfy women customers who insist upon his trying to perfectly and comfortably fit dainty shoes to their large feet. One may be a king or queen or a servant or a pauper. High or low, exalted or humble, man is a spiritual being! So long as he can think he can always change the outer, or physical, effects to suit the desire of his heart. And the very first steps lie in the thought and in the feeling!

PUPIL: When one's whole environment is one of poverty, or illness, or other dark limitations, how can one have beautiful and hopeful thoughts? Is it not true that the environment influences one's thoughts and feelings? While one is forced to live in the same adverse environment I do not see how there can be much change.

MASTER: If one were perfectly satisfied with an environment such as you describe there could not, and would not, be any change. But if one were divinely dissatisfied with such conditions, and very much wished to change them, it may be done any time, as completely as one may wish, by resort to and use of the Laws of Life. Suppose, for example, that you would like a position that is more agreeable, more lucrative, shorter hours, etc. If you go forth to look for such a "job," by all means start out with the feeling that you have something valuable to GIVE an employer, and not go out to see how much you can get. If you GIVE the getting will automatically follow. Carry the light of God-consciousness with you in seeking betterment of your position; and when you approach your prospective employer let the light shine. Suppose too, that you wish a better, more comfortable house in which to live. The very fact that you desire this change is PROOF POSITIVE that it is for you to have IF you will meet the requirements. Many persons try to bring harmony into a home by getting a larger and better home, or by changing companions, by moving into another community.

PUPIL: That would help, would it not?

MASTER: Temporarily it might. But it would in no sense endure. To attempt to bring happiness or freedom into one's life through outward changes only is not wisdom, is not true art. Such is misuse of the divine materials. The change must occur within, and within first! It must first be established in mind, and firmly enthroned there if it is to be other than only temporarily effective. As long as a trend of thought remains the same the result will be the same. The LAW OF LIFE IS:

TO CHANGE AN EFFECT THE CAUSE MUST BE CHANGED FIRST. CAUSE LEADS; EFFECTS FOLLOW! THOUGHT IS THE CAUSE; CONDITIONS ARE THE EFFECTS!

PUPIL: Does one's longing for beautiful surroundings, for health and freedom, for a lovely picture in perfect balance, come from the Great Artist who has made all of Nature? Is it He painting His ideal picture for us on the canvas of our individual minds?

MASTER: Yes, God is Mind, Life, Intelligence, Power, Beauty, Love, Harmony, etc. If any of these things are desired by us, and they are, then surely the Creator of them all must have planted that thought-seed in the mind. He must have whispered into that mental ear and that spiritual heart that THE TRUTH IS YOURS! God has chosen YOU as a holy instrument through which to manifest all of His beautiful and wonderful qualities of Life. It is the DIVINE ORDER and WILL that YOU should manifest that particular thing, that particular place in Life!

4

God-Consciousness Versus Sense-Consciousness

PUPIL: Then if our truly fine desires are the desires of God Himself trying to manifest in and through us as individuals, in some particular way, why are there so many misfits in life? Why are there so very few who are doing, really doing, just what they would like to do? Why are there so very, very few living the life they truly wish to live? Why? Why? Why? Surely God can fulfill His own desires.

MASTER: Unless ALL things are possible to God then nothing is possible to Him. God has projected each human forth from Himself, each of us possessing an individual mind, for the sole purpose of manifesting Himself and His glory through us. Verily the MIND of man IS the SON of God! The Son has been given absolute liberty. Each can always make of his life, for a time at least, whatsoever he may choose. Man already possesses everything that God had to give him! Each person can make or mar his own picture, exactly as he wishes. By nature man is free to draw from the Ever-Present Parent Mind anything, and all things, that he requires to fulfill his desires. If this is not true then God's highest creation, man, is a mere nothing, an automatic something like a clock which when once wound will run until it runs down. Man IS, however, God's own idea in flesh. The Intelligent Life in man is man's Divine Father! Man is already perfect and complete, IS made of the same essence as his Father (God)!

There is only one reason why every mortal does not manifest and reproduce the Life, Love and Beauty which we see brought out in such radiance and perfection in all of Nature, manifested in Nature to the extreme point where mechanical and automatic actions can bring them. But we as individuals have a Law of Being that is somewhat different in one way from that which governs the other creatures that are of the world we call Nature. For us that are human the only perfect reproduction of Life, Love, Power and Beauty that we can ever know must come from Liberty. That is to say we have freedom of choice that is commensurate with that of the Originating Life-Spirit Itself. In other words we as individuals have the LIBERTY of accepting or rejecting either good or evil, exactly as we may choose them. And the choice that we make results from the state of our consciousness. If we are God-conscious, we ARE gods. But if we are sense-conscious only, then we are creatures of darkness, of illness, of poverty, of loneliness, and all other things that are undesirable. "Choose ye well, therefore, whom ye will serve!" God-consciousness or sense-consciousness, which?

PUPIL: You have given us a powerful and illuminating "dose" here. Already we have a whole lesson. But I still do not see why God's highest creation, man should ever reject any of the good things of life.

MASTER: IF man really understood the Law of his own Being, he never should reject the good things. But there are FEW who fully understand this Law, which is a wide-open door to ABSOLUTE FREEDOM! Most people believe that the "law of their being"

(purposely spelled without capital letters) is a law of limitation rather than a LAW OF ABSOLUTE LIBERTY! Man "does not expect to find the starting point of the Creative Process reproduced in himself; so he looks to the mechanical side of things for the basis of his reasoning about Life.

Consequently his reasoning leads him to the conclusion that Life is limited because he has assumed limitation as his premise; and so, logically, he can not escape from it (limitation) in his conclusion." Here in this wonderful quotation from Troward you have the WHOLE STORY of limitation. Here Troward shows most clearly that is all a MATTER OF CONSCIOUSNESS! And so the tragedy results because man in his dense ignorance ridicules the idea of TRANSCENDING the law of limitation, forgetting completely (if indeed he ever learned it) that THE LAW can include all of the lower laws so fully as to completely swallow them!

PUPIL: From what you say it would seem that man's only reason for knowing limitation of any kind is his own lack of understanding. Is man to blame because he does not know?

MASTER: No man is to blame for what he does not know. But surely all persons will suffer because of NOT USING WHAT THEY DO KNOW! And they shall keep right on suffering until, like small children, they learn from experience.

PUPIL: It seems "strange," to say the least, that each of us must learn to find his own fuller Life in his own way. Why did not God COMPEL His idea (man) to understand from birth that Life is Joy, and Joy is Freedom, etc.?

MASTER: Please THINK for just a minute! Would there be ANY FREEDOM, ANY LIBERTY, in that kind of person? Such an individual should be a mere automaton with no sense of LIBERTY at all! God forbid that any of us, His children, become robots!

PUPIL: It seems to me that most people feel life is entirely made up of a constant round of prosaic and homely activities which we are obliged to follow: To the shop, or office we go. We toil and slave, and go home again, all worn out and cranky. We sleep, maybe, then arise to repeat it all again for years until in God's mercy we die. There can be no real joy in that kind of life; but to most of mankind that is all. Still this is NOT all, is it?

MASTER: Indeed that is NOT all, not even for the darkest and most limited of persons. However dark, spiritually and materially, a person may be, deep down in his soul there is a conviction that Life holds his desires fulfilled somehow, somewhere, sometime! He feels also that IF HE ONLY KNEW HOW HE COULD FIND A WAY! Some feel that the real joy of LIBERTY can come only after putting off the body at death. This is NOT the case, however, EVERYTHING THAT LIFE (GOD) HAS TO GIVE IS HERE IN OUR MIDST, AND RIGHT NOW!

As we humans advance in knowledge, either from study or experience, or both, we overcome one law of limitation after another BY FINDING THE HIGHER AND GREATER LAW of which all lower laws are but PARTIAL expressions. At length we see clearly before us, as our ultimate goal, this Truth: "Nothing less than the PERFECT LAW OF LIBERTY -not liberty without Law, which is anarchy -but LIBERTY ACCORDING TO LAW!" When man learns the Law of his own Being, he will specialize it in all of his ways and will have found his true place. Thus will he bring INTO FORM all of the desires of his heart; then will he know the REAL ART OF LIVING!

PUPIL: Can anyone who will learn from Life, either by study or experience, that the Creative Energy, with ALL that it has to give, is an Ever-Present, Responsive Quality of Life? Then can one really materialize, really bring into outward form, his most secret and sacred desires! That would be the art of living sure enough.

MASTER: THE LAW OF LIFE IS CHANGELESS FOREVER! It is always calling to you in these words, or in ones like them: "Come unto ME! Learn about ME! Through ME ALL things are possible unto you because WE, YOU and I, are eternally ONE! I am LIFE! I am Creative; I am always Responsive to the thoughts and emotions with which I am impressed by you! I am MIND! The Law of Mind is MY law! Because this is true it is Truth also that 'AS YOU THINK IN YOUR HEART SO ARE YOU!' Thinking GIVES FORM to the UNformed Life!"

PUPIL: This is splendid! But again it is getting "heavy." May we have another personal illustration of the adaptation of this principle to everyday living as people live it? This will help, I am sure.

MASTER: All right; I am always happy to comply with such requests if they will really help you. I once knew a dentist, a very fine dentist and a good man. He confided to me one day that music was his very life, and not prosaic dentistry. He said that he was weary of being "down in the mouth all of the time."

"So," I asked, "you feel that you are not in your right place?"

"I know that I am not!" he replied.

"Just why aren't you in your right groove?" I queried.

"Because music will not yield me enough money to keep my family in anything like moderate comfort. I feel that marriage and a family are among Life's deepest joys and greatest blessings. But music is like politics; one has to have lots of 'pull' to get into the few places that will really pay for a good violinist."

"Are you sure of that?" I asked.

"Yes, quite!"

"Well, Mr. Dentist," I said, "I know a God who is All-Intelligent, All-Powerful, Ever-present, Ever-Responsive and Forever Creative! HE is also the Greatest of Master Artists, the Real Maestro! He lives forever deep within your own soul. If you will try going into Him there, if you will establish Harmony there, and will know and understand the Beauty which your music must express there, and if you will be content only with perfection there and in your music, I KNOW that you can and will reap all the reward that any one can wish for in music, just as in any other profession, art or business."

"Your words cause my hopes to soar," he said. "But how can one like me, one who knows very little about God, contact Him?"

"Go within yourself! Go through, or beneath, the confusing, bewildering, disheartening past experiences. Live wholly in and enjoy only the harmonious side of your nature, which is wise, beautiful and most powerful in all ways. Then practice, practice, practice putting that INNER Beauty and Harmony into vibration through the strings of your violin."

"But I am too old to take this up now."

"Not at all! Loving music as you do, you have kept up with your practice, have you not? Then DO TRY WHAT I HAVE TOLD YOU! Try it with faith and love in your heart. Hold them there with a determination and pride which simply will not surrender."

The dentist continued to find excuses, many of them, like so many people do, tragically enough. He did not have time, nor did he feel like it, after long, hard days at the office. He should have to give some time to his family, must have some recreation, etc., etc. But I did not hear him. I kept right on singing glowing word-notes for him, tempting him to try hard, inspiring him with courage. When he stopped finding excuses, and seemed really interested, he asked for the exact method to use. I told him the following steps:

(1)   First, he must thoroughly make up his mind that his love for music, his deep passion for the expression of harmony was no accident; he must know that it was nothing less than God Himself persistently, relentlessly urging for expression through him.

(2)   He should go carefully over and recite to himself the Lord's prayer, quietly but with much love and feeling, not less than twice every day, each night upon retiring and each morning when he first awakened.

(3)   He should faithfully VISUALIZE himself playing, playing, playing, joyfully, harmoniously, enthusiastically playing to large and most appreciative audiences, receiving really handsome checks for his concerts, etc.

(4)   After his periods of visualizing he should faithfully use some affirmation that appealed to him, that would strengthen his faith when it sagged, that would feed his high resolve, that would fan his burning urge to a holy flame.

(5)   He should practice, practice, PRACTICE his music, striving always with all of his heart and soul to do much better with each rendition than he had ever done before.

Within less than one year the dentist became the musician! He was making more from his "pot boiler" concerts than he had ever made at dentistry. Within another half-year he began a national concert-tour which within a few months yielded him enough to go to Europe for additional study for two years, and to have his family with him over there. Since that time he has done nothing, professionally, but play his violin. He has not, of course, accumulated a really great fortune, but he and his loved ones have all of the good things of life that they wish, and this, combined with an abiding sense of happiness, constitutes TRUE WEALTH for any person!

PUPIL: Does this same plan apply to everyone, and the same steps?

MASTER: The SAME PRINCIPLES apply to all! The exact plan, and the steps that lead to its fulfillment, will vary a little, of course, with each specific case. But no matter what your big desire may be, your Father's dearest wish for you is the absolute fulfillment of that desire by you, by you in partnership with Him! He always LONGS to give you any and all good things! His WHOLE PURPOSE in having created you was that He MIGHT EXPRESS HIMSELF THROUGH YOU! THIS IS EXACTLY WHY HE CREATED INDIVIDUALS, and THIS IS WHY HE DOES LIVE IN AND THROUGH THEM! If we would have any of His GIFTS AS OUR VERY OWN we need ONLY to LIFT UP OUR FALLEN CONSCIOUSNESS TO THIS HOLY BELIEF and THEN WORK IN SHEER JOY AND EXPECTATION towards the LOVELY VISION WE HAVE IN VIEW!

5

Personal Intimacy With God

PUPIL: Please tell me a definite way to get closer to God, to push the little love and understanding that I have further into the Great Oneness until my limited vision is completely absorbed in the Unlimited. Will you do this just for me?

MASTER: Gladly. Since this is your own book, you may take all the time that you require, and at such intervals as you please, to study it, then study it still some more, and to practice it until you have really mastered it and made it a part of your very self. The very best way to completely sublimate your human self, your sense self with all of its limitations, into the INFINITE is to establish within yourself a PERSONAL INTIMACY WITH GOD!

PUPIL: But can this be done? Do you mean to say that we may actually be on terms of personal intimacy with God, as with a friend or other loved one? Such a thing seems too good to be true, too strange and mysterious to believe.

MASTER: Yes, this can be done. In fact it is done in each of us at all times whether or not we are aware of it. Remember always that each of us was made by, and out of the same stuff as, the Ever-Present, Intelligent, Creative Life Itself. Each of us was fashioned out of It Itself; and each of us IS It Itself in a physical form. This being so, it automatically follows that each of us is always in a MOST PERSONAL INTIMACY with God! God IS our Maker, our very life, our body, our thoughts, our desires, our everything!

PUPIL: Then why are there any troubles at all in this world? Why is not the lot of every person peace, joy and perfection at all times?

MASTER: That question I have answered a number of times, in one form or another. But yet once again let me say that it is all a matter of each individual's own CONSCIOUSNESS. Our thoughts make us what we are! The whole shape of our lives, and of what we call "conditions," take their form FROM OUR MOST HABITUAL THOUGHT AND FEELING! Don't ever lose sight of this outstandingly important fact. The Originating Creative Power is UNformed relative to your individual life UNTIL IT FLOWS THROUGH YOUR THOUGHT! It is throughout CONSTANT AWARENESS of the truth that God IS ever-resident within us, IS forever flowing through us as thought, that we are lifted right out of the old, limited habits of judging everything from external appearances, or from sense-consciousness only.

PUPIL: But I still do not quite see how this awareness will change the whole life from darkness to light. Just how will it do it?

MASTER: If you are CONSTANTLY AWARE of the fact that YOU REALLY ARE GOD HIMSELF in miniature, that you ARE always on terms of personal intimacy with Him as with your own self, then you will not any longer think thoughts that are unlike Him. You will not think thoughts of limitation of any nature; you will not judge anything or anybody from the standpoint of sense-consciousness. And when you have changed your Thoughts and Feelings to the point where you are HABITUALLY THINKING ONLY FROM THE SPIRITUAL

SIDE OF THINGS you will readily discover that to really KNOW GOD IS TO BE GOD! Then indeed are you in constant personal intimacy with God; and you will leave far behind you the dismal bogs of failure, lack, disease, loneliness and despair. You will emerge into, and abide securely in, the GREEN PASTURES of the fulfillment of your every treasured desire!

Persist, persist and yet again persist, in your steady recognition of the Truth that the actual purpose of the Divine in having projected YOU into being from its own Bosom was this and this ONLY: That it might

CONTINUALLY FLOW THROUGH YOU AS CONSCIOUSNESS, and that it might always SPECIALIZE IN YOU AS HEALTH, WEALTH, PEACE AND JOY! Through this realization you lift your thought and feeling above limitations, and this is the solution to every problem. Yes, through the radiant gate of PERSONAL INTIMACY WITH GOD we step into a NEW WORLD in which ALL IS LIFE AND LIBERTY! Truly God IS an EVERPRESENT EVERYWHERE ALL-THE-TIME, LOVING, RESPONSIVE, CREATIVE POWER!

PUPIL: Since you often encourage us to use the Bible as a standard and a way-shower, can you refer us to a place in the Bible in which we are given a means of establishing this conscious personal intimacy with God?

MASTER: Certainly. The Bible is replete with illustrations of this very principle. For instance, let's turn to St. Matthew, Chapter 22, verses 36, 37, 38, 39 and 40; and note what Jesus, the Greatest of all Great Teachers, says there. Let us study it and analyze it carefully. Here it is:

(a)   Verse 36: "Master, what is the GREAT COMMANDMENT in the Law?" This question, asked of Jesus by the lawyer, was one of vital importance; and in the answer that Jesus gave is the GOLDEN KEY that millions desire. Note the reply below:

(b)   Verses 37 and 38: "Jesus said unto him: 'Thou shalt LOVE the Lord thy God with ALL THY HEART, and with ALL THY SOUL, and with ALL THY MIND! THIS is the FIRST and GREAT commandment." Kindly note very carefully, and ponder deeply, the THREE steps that are united into ONE through His use of the word "LOVE." The heart, the soul and the mind constitute ALL of the SPIRITUAL BEING! Hence if we really love God with ALL of our heart and soul and mind, we are in fact loving Him with ALL OF OUR ALL! Is this not true? Indeed it IS! Here then we have Jesus' own way, His own method, of establishing within Himself PERSONAL INTIMACY WITH GOD!

(c)   Verses 39 and 40 read thus: "And the second (commandment) is like unto it (like unto the first one) Thou shalt LOVE THY NEIGHBOR AS THYSELF! On these TWO commandments hang ALL the LAW and the prophets." Please observe here the tremendous importance that Jesus places upon loving our neighbors as we love our own selves. There are many who pay lip-service to this Divine injunction, and who profess that they really DO love their neighbors as themselves. But when it comes to the crucial test of dividing their possessions in love with a less fortunate neighbor, or of going to any extremity of "trouble" for him, their protestations of love for the neighbors are far too often found to be only mere words, shallow and empty and vain. So remember this: in words WITHOUT DEEDS TO SUPPORT THEM there is NO VIRTUE! It is a FACT that our neighbors (every last one of them) are as precious in the sight of God as we are; in truth our neighbors are an integral part of ourselves, in other forms. It is a FACT also that we can not really love God unless we love our neighbor; and it is a still greater TRUTH that if we DO love our neighbor as we love our self we are loving God. God is ONE! Yet most of us make the tragic mistake of thinking that God is many, that our neighbor is one person and we another, etc. The DIVINE REALITY, however, is that ALL PEOPLE (yes every last one of the millions and millions on earth) are ONE BODY UNIFIED FOREVER IN GOD! This being so, it is impossible for us to help a neighbor (who is our self) without also helping ourselves. Neither can we criticize, condemn or injure a neighbor (who is our self) without doing ourselves greater harm than is done to the neighbor. In PERSONAL INTIMACY WITH GOD there is, in reality NO "neighbor" and NO "self," as two persons, as ones separate and apart from each other; rather each of us is also all other persons, and all other persons are our own selves! When the dwellers on earth learn this all-important lesson that Jesus taught, and when all persons are obedient to this Law, then we shall have the Millennium here in our midst -then will all of us be veritable angels of the ONE DIVINE BODY!

PUPIL: This is a most beautiful and powerful illustration. In addition to studying about it and thinking about it what else should we do about it?

MASTER: The most important thing of all is to PRACTICE it, to LIVE it! Otherwise there is no virtue in it at all. If you can accept these words of Jesus as Truth, then ALLY yourself with them in your THOUGHT and FEELING and ACTIONS, then will your whole being be fed with spiritual MANNA. You will be given constant suggestions by the Spirit regarding the sanest and most fruitful methods of living your own personal life in TRUE UNITY WITH GOD.

PUPIL: And will this not develop still more in us that great essential to which you gave such importance in Lesson Number One, namely a good disposition?

MASTER: Indeed it will! And no age in all of history has ever more needed to learn and practice this great lesson of GROWTH, DEVELOPMENT and true ENRICHMENT than the people of today. Many read the Truth; few assimilate it! Many hear the Truth; few heed it! Many know the Truth; FEW DO IT! That is exactly why there is a real MASTER only at long and rare intervals. The price of MASTERY is really easy; but it is so much contrary to sense-consciousness (out of which all selfishness is born) that FEW have the courage, the faith and the spiritual stamina, and the LOVE, to try it earnestly, or to stick to it through outward confusion, until it HAS BEEN PROVED!

PUPIL: Is there any other method you can think of that will help us to understand this Great Law still better? Are there any short cuts? In the study I mean, not in the practice of it?

MASTER: Yes, there are short-cuts from which a truly observant and intelligent person may find this Law actually fulfilled in beautiful harmony, and from which we humans may learn a very great deal, if we will. Perhaps the greatest of these shortcuts to ILLUMINATION is the one that is most widely distributed, and to which every last soul has access in one form or another, and with very little "trouble" if they sincerely wish to seek it out. I mean NATURE, of course. ALL of Nature shows forth the GLORY OF LIVING IN CONSTANT PERSONAL INTIMACY WITH GOD!

By way of example of what I mean, let us briefly study the four seasons of the year, and the reaction of Nature to each. Spring in all of Nature is the period of IMMORTALITY expressed anew, and in wonderful splendor! It is the season of budding, of flowering, of mating, of Generation and of Re-generation, all of which are among the HOLIEST of the functions of Nature. And mark well how all of Dame Nature's children are always OBEDIENT to the urge of Spring, to the sublime song of the Spirit! Only men are rebellious to the holy commands of the Spirit; and it appears quite obvious that only men sin. How long will it be before we who are human awaken to the TRUE GLORY that is OUR DIVINE BIRTHRIGHT?

In the realm of Nature summer is the time when fruits are formed, developed and ripened in fulfillment of the Law of the Spirit. It is the season when seeds are formed within the fruits so that with the coming of another spring all of Nature may obey again the great injunction found so often in the account of Creation in Genesis, namely; "Be ye fruitful and multiply, and fill the face of the earth with fruit."

With the autumn comes the PRECIOUS HARVEST, the time when the radiant PROMISE that was given in the spring is FULFILLED IN FORM, just as every promise of the Spirit to US will surely be manifested in form in our lives, and with a most bountiful harvest, IF only we humans will learn to OBEY the Spirit without question, as do the fair children of Nature, and cease our foolish rebellion that is the one and only source of all of our afflictions!

Then follows the winter and Nature RESTS from its labors of the spring, summer and fall, just as we also must have our periods of rest. But winter positively is NOT aging, or decadence, or death, not in Nature. It is the season of rest, of slumber, only. But if you want to think that winter is the symbol of "death," as some people insist upon doing, I will agree with you for a minute solely for the purpose of pointing out the FALLACY of death, or the belief in death, as clearly revealed by Nature. In winter Nature does APPEAR dead. BUT IS IT DEAD? By no means! With the first few warm days of spring the LIFE which has been merely SOMNOLENT in Nature, (but which has NOT perished because it can NOT perish, not ever) again RESPONDS! The buds, animated anew by the vitality of the Spirit, swell and burst; and the leaves and flowers that were HIDDEN from view (but THERE nevertheless) come harmoniously, joyously forth in their beauty and glory to express IMMORTALITY! As Nature DOES so may MAN DO ALSO if he only will. IF YOU WOULD KNOW TRUE ILLUMINATION, and the POWER and the GLORY that are born of it, GO THOU TO NATURE! STUDY HER WAYS AND BE WISE! STUDY HER WAYS AND REALLY LIVE!

6

Individuality

(What Is the Truth about the Individual and His Individuality?)

MASTER: Have you ever given thought to the matter of HOW you came into existence? Are you convinced that there was, and is, a DEFINITE PURPOSE in the Divine Mind to account for your being here on earth? Or do you think that you create the purpose of your life for yourself, independently of all other factors, after you come into this world?

PUPIL: You ask questions that I scarcely know how to answer. These questions have perhaps been of mild and brief interest to me in the past; but I have never given them any real thought. I have let my mind wander as concerns these points. One time I would think that the Creative Parent Mind does have a definite purpose in my being here, and that this being so there is no use in my trying to change things. But it would then occur to me that this conception of things would mean the "pre-destination" of the fundamentalists. So I would change my mind and decide that I must have some hand in determining my mental and spiritual progress. Is this right?

MASTER: Indeed you do have a hand in your self-development. You have a VERY GREAT PART in it! The life that is you as an individual came directly out of the Great Whole of Intelligent Life (God), from out of its very own sacred heart-center. Your very life is the Spirit's GIFT OF ITS OWN SELF TO YOU! Secondly, the Divine DID have a specific purpose in having made you namely: That it might have a NEW FORM, a new center, through which it might operate as THOUGHT and FEELING, and through which it might yet more fully

ENJOY ITSELF in a particular way. This also is the Spirit's GIFT OF ITS OWN SELF TO YOU! BUT the manner in which you as an individual use these HOLY GIFTS is left entirely in your hands, without interference from the Spirit. You were given other holy boons; you were given INITIATIVE and SELECTION; you were given absolute FREEDOM OF CHOICE! The distance that you travel towards the goal of spiritual perfection in this earth life depends solely upon YOU, just as the degree of rapidity with which you may mentally grow is entirely up to YOU!

PUPIL: But are we not given certain divine urges, or longings at all stages of our lives which will help us to know the right way to go? Are we not given these certain desires, or impulses, or stimuli?

MASTER: Certainly. And unless one follows these Divine impulses one is never really quite satisfied, one is always restless, always feels that some essential is lacking, that his right place eludes him. Your very individuality is an EXACT COMPLEMENT of the Great Whole, is a specialized action of all of Life. The only difference in the Life, the Love, the Beauty or the Power of the Universal (God) and of the individual (man), as expressed through the

Universal and the individual, is a difference in SCALE. THE QUALITY OF THE TWO (which in reality are but ONE) IS EXACTLY The SAME!

The very same Creator who made and directs the whole universe also made and will direct you, if you will let Him do so, because HE HIMSELF LIVES IN YOU as the Life of you. His infinite Creative Power and Intelligent Love are the VERY SAME IN YOU that they are in all other created things. Therefore it is not just sentiment to say and feel and KNOW, as did Jesus: 'THE FATHER (God) AND I ARE ONE! THE FATHER IN ME, HE DOETH THE WORK!" If only we will develop a constant recognition of this most profound Truth, we shall then really HAVE an abiding sense of LIBERTY, of LIBERTY IN UNION, of LIBERTY IN CONSCIOUS UNION WITH ALL OF LIFE! This is not just an idle but beautiful rhapsody; it is a simple, but most powerful and illuminating, STATEMENT OF FACT!

PUPIL: Am I right then in believing that if I could really think myself into an unshakeable conviction that God IS ever-present in me, and that ALL of His Creative Power is MINE to draw from at my own will and pleasure, I could accomplish ANYTHING and EVERYTHING that I might wish, and could BE and HAVE whatsoever I might desire?

MASTER: Yes, you are right. The Creative Power of God in us is UNformed with respect to what we may wish to accomplish until we ourselves give it definite direction with our thought and feeling. It is ALWAYS RESPONSIVE, remember, to any and all of our thoughts and feelings. These things being true, and they ARE true, any person may BE, DO and HAVE whatsoever that one may desire, IF, of course, one ACTIVELY WORKS in a corresponding direction. It is logic, it is purest gospel, that there is no other way than the one that Life's true purpose in us is to be forever seeking to express itself through us as FREEDOM! Remember always, I urge you, that our THOUGHTS and FEELINGS DO BECOME THINGS, and that they determine the shape that the unformed substance of the Spirit takes in its living expression in our individual lives. It is, as Troward says, like water flowing through a pipe; the water always assumes the shape and the size of the pipe through which it is sent. It is like harnessed electricity which always manifests in exact correspondence with the kind of instrument through which it passes as it works. It the light-bulb the electricity ACTUALLY BECOMES light; in the doorbell it rings the bell; in the refrigerator it generates cold; in the stove it becomes heat. It is the same electricity, the same Power, in every case; and the instrument through which it passes determines what the Power is and what it does! Once a person truly grasps the real meaning of the Spirit's Principles, then one realizes fully that we as individuals are actually sent out from the very Heart of God Himself in order that we may BECOME and BE new and perfect centers through which HE can operate in JOY, in ever-increasing JOY.

This and this only, is the will of God towards us! Yes, the exalted mission of each of us is that we may be new instruments for DIVINE EXPRESSION. If we will to become that, and will make the necessary mental and physical effort to realize this Truth, then we will KNOW that we ARE filling our right place in life. We shall experience true and lasting happiness then because we SHALL BE DOING the things we MOST ENJOY DOING. There will be an ever present-sense of GROWTH in our lives also. Only a very few individuals have ever reached this empyrean height in consciousness while on the earth-plane; STILL IT IS POSSIBLE TO ALL. Because so few attain this exalted level most people have the merest existence, one that is filled with seemingly continual and perplexing problems of one sort or another.

PUPIL: It seems to me there are many more people who are unhappy here than happy ones. So many of my personal friends feel themselves to be misfits in life, I do not think that I know even one person, including myself, who is perfectly happy. If one has health, as some do, then that one may have financial troubles. If they do not have financial worries, and no real physical woes, then they have family discord. And so on it goes until one wonders if there is such a thing as complete happiness in this phase of existence.

MASTER: You are right; and the real reason for all of this unrest is this: These individuals have not recognized that their THOUGHTS and FEELINGS are the ONLY INSTRUMENTS by which the All-

Creative Energy CAN manifest in their lives. It is of no avail to blame Providence, or other people, for your troubles. No matter what form chaotic conditions take in your life YOU ALONE ARE RESPONSIBLE FOR THEM; and YOU ALONE CAN RECTIFY THEM through use of your inseverable contact with God. Once one learns through study and practice, or through experience, TO ALLOW the WILL OF GOD (which is always GOOD) TO HAVE FREE ACTION IN AND THROUGH HIM, then ALL BONDAGE TO CONDITIONS IS OVER!

PUPIL: At the risk of appearing dull may I ask yet again just how this can be done by each of us?

MASTER: I have given you the answer a number of times in this book; but it is worth repeating in a little different form, for it is an ALLIMPORTANT item. Here is the answer yet again:

(1)   Mentally go deep within your inmost self, your own Divine inmost, and ask yourself: "What DOES God really mean to me?" "What must the Divine Nature in me be like?"

(2)   Once you have formed a definite and positive conclusion on these points, try to reproduce this same feeling all through your whole being. KEEP TRYING, and you will succeed in doing it. It is worth the effort required, a million times over.

(3)   Do NOT let yourself be discouraged with this practice if you do not seem to get immediate results. Remember always that Troward says "it is the intention that counts; it is the intention which registers on the reproductive disk of Creative Life."

(4)   Another powerful help, to me personally at least, is to diligently use that affirmation from Troward which begins: "My mind IS a center of Divine

operation," etc. (See "Your Invisible Power," or Troward's "Dore Lectures"). The Lord's Prayer is also an excellent aid, as I have repeatedly written herein.

(5)   Try, try, try with all of your concentrated purpose to LIVE HOURLY in the FEELING of the affirmation, or the prayer. Do NOT let yourself slip and fall by indulgence in what you may call "justifiable impatience" for there is no such thing. Anger, or jealousy, or fear, and all like things, will cause you to slip also, for these things are unlike your idea of God, or of God's thought.

PUPIL: That is a very tall order!

MASTER: Not when you realize constantly that it is the intention that counts. The more you keep your intention right the less frequently will you slip in your practice of these principles; and soon your whole life shall have been altered until it IS like your own conception of God.

PUPIL: Many people who seem to have a very good idea of Christian Science, Divine Science, Unity, etc., try very hard for more money, better health, higher social position. Yet they do not seem to get far. Why?

MASTER: Whether or not they are conscious of it they are looking to the outside as the source from which these things shall come to them. But the ORIGIN OF ALL GOOD THINGS IS WITHIN! All good is WITHIN your own Life-Stream; and this MUST BE RECOGNIZED! Our recognition of the WITHIN, the Spiritual, as the TRUE SOURCE of all good things WILL GIVE THEM FORM in the OUTER or physical, WORLD in which we live. Once the contact is made WITHIN, and faithfully held, the things will AUTOMATICALLY come to pass in the outer. The whole secret is this: We MUST know exactly WHO we are, WHAT we are and WHY we are! Knowing this, our contact with the SOURCE OF ALL GOOD is never interrupted. It is our task to take care of the INNER things; and if we do, the outer things SHALL TAKE CARE OF THEMSELVES. THEN SHALL WE

GO FORWARD, AND ONLY FORWARD, HAPPILY, HARMONIOUSLY, SERENELY ACCOMPLISHING ANY AND ALL GOOD THINGS THAT WE MAY WISH!

7

Personal Pointers On Success

MASTER: No one ever slides into real success without personal effort. It takes all one has to attain unto real success, and to hold it: but by the very same law each person HAS ALL IT TAKES! If we are willing to reach out for achievement, and to use all of our faculties to that end, then unqualified, constant success is surely ours. It has been said that Napoleon never blundered into a victory. He always won his battles IN HIS MIND before he won them on the field. This is exactly what every successful person does!

PUPIL: What is the very first step on the high road to success?

MASTER: The very first step is to DECIDE definitely and positively what form of success you want. Henry Ford, for example, wished with all of his heart and soul to make BETTER AUTOMOBILES

CHEAPER, cars that were within the financial reach of all persons. Thomas A. Edison wanted to provide various efficient electrical appliances at moderate prices for the convenience and comfort of the world. Jesus the Christ had one outstanding desire ever-present in His consciousness: To SHOW THE WAY for every human being to find the Father-Principle within himself, to show all how to find and know and trust that Infinite Divine Power which really will, and DOES, protect all, guide all, provide for all. Each of these men had a divine urge that burned within him, an all-consuming passion to do one thing better than it may have been done before. Because they KNEW EXACTLY WHAT THEY MOST WISHED TO DO THEY DID IT!

PUPIL: If one does not know exactly what line of endeavor to pursue, what is a good thing to look for in determining just what is best to do?

MASTER: Here is another most-important essential to success; this will give you your cue. The MORE GOOD a person CAN DO FOR OTHERS with his product, his life, his work, or whatever it may be, the GREATER SUCCESS will that person have! No one ever succeeded in any very great degree whose dominant motive was that of personal gain only. If one actually helps others, many others, to live happier, better, more successful lives, one need give little thought to the gain that will accompany the success; for if one does this the gain to self can not possibly be withheld. One's chief motive then in reaching out for success is not to see how much he may help himself but to see how greatly he may help many others.

PUPIL: These two steps are most helpful to me. But before taking other steps may I ask just what pitfalls I should look out for most when first I start on the road?

MASTER: Here are two of the most common snares, I think:

1. Never yet has success come, and never shall it come, to any person who simply wishes for it. Mere wishes are idle and utterly impotent unless the wish

is great enough to INSPIRE ONE TO IMMEDIATE ACTION. Yes, ACTION, not wishes, is the BIG THING.

2. Keeping your mind centered on the big success that you "are going to be" will NEVER bring it to pass. You must KNOW yourself successful NOW. So long as one looks upon success as a FUTURE acquirement just so long will success be POSTPONED, just so long will its attainment always remain FUTURE. From the very start one must learn to BACK UP the THOUGHT with the FEELING, the absolute conviction, that I AM SUCCESS NOW!

PUPIL: These are splendid, too. Now I am ready for another step forward.

MASTER: Since you have now firmly resolved to make a business of acquiring true success in accordance with Life's immutable Laws, you must throw your whole energy into making your mind a center for positive thoughts only, for constructive thoughts only. You are deliberately careful of the words you use. You are deliberately careful of your mental reaction to the words you may hear. For instance, if you hear people talking about a tornado you should not let your thoughts dwell upon destruction but rather upon tremendous power POSITIVELY used. If you hear people talking about disease, you should inwardly know that while disease is a natural result of broken natural laws it is not necessarily evil, and that in Life as Life ALL IS GOOD AND PERFECT. In a word it will be necessary for you to avoid all detours, even though they may appear easy and short.

PUPIL: What are some of these detours? How will they be marked?

MASTER: All of them should be marked with lots of red lanterns for certainly they are dangerous to one seeking success. Here are a few of them which you will recognize as questions that you have asked yourself, just as millions of other Truth-seekers; and yet they wonder why success always eludes them.

1. "Well, WHY doesn't it come?"

2. "WHEN will it come?"

3. "MAYBE this is the way it will come."

4. "Perhaps it is not God's will that I have this."

Success does not come for the one who asks: "Well, why doesn't it come?" simply because he is asking WHY rather than KNOWING that IT NOW IS! For the one who whimpers: "When will it come?" it shall never come so long as he asks WHEN. What they wish NOW IS or else it never will be. And as concerns "God's will" for us His will for us is anything good we may desire.

PUPIL: Just why is it that if we wish success for ourselves only, for personal gain only, we shall not be apt to get it?

MASTER: Here is an illustration. Suppose you went to your own personal banker and asked him for a loan of one hundred thousand dollars, knowing that he had that much, and more to loan and that your worth justified a loan of that amount. No doubt his first question would be that one that bankers always ask first of anybody seeking a loan, i.e., "What do you want the money for?" Let's suppose you answered: "Oh, I wish to take a year's cruise on my yacht, doing nothing, just loafing, resting, sleeping; eating. I need the change, you see." Do you think he would let you have the money? No not a soul! No more will the Great Universal Banker (God) under like, or similar, circumstances. You must approach Him with a really good idea, one which will bring good to many, not just to yourself. I know men who have millions and who began with no money, who began only with an idea. Their basic ideas were so universal towards the production of good they were able to secure from others all the money necessary to finance the beginning of their enterprises. The great secret of individual success is the very same as that of the national success that has made America the wealthiest land on earth, and is this: Our men of affairs, of greatest success, have learned to share with all of our people through benefiting all of the people, either directly or indirectly, through dispensing higher quality goods at less cost, through sharing earnings more generously with employees, etc. They have learned that it is an absolute science that giving to and sharing with many always have getting as a natural correlative! Get your thought right; capture an idea that will prove helpful to many; then DRAW IN CONFIDENCE on the Unlimited Banker for all that you require. You will discover that you cannot keep money from gravitating to you. Herein lies SURE and CONTINUING SUCCESS!

PUPIL: May we have here, in conclusion, the gist of this whole matter of true success, in summary form? This will facilitate ready reference by us who are students.

MASTER: Certainly you may have this. It may be said that the steps to success are seven in number; and here they are:

1. Thoroughly make up your mind exactly what you want most right now.

2. Be certain that your desire has in it the element of good for many. Then ask your own inmost soul for the most perfect idea, or ideas, relative to your desire, ideas that will PRODUCE GOOD FOR MANY.

3. Make a mental picture of your desire as FULFILLED NOW, and NOW only, making the mental picture complete, vivid, alive with feeling. This is the meaning of Jesus' great statement to "ASK BELIEVING THAT YOU (ALREADY) HAVE." In the mental picture you ACTUALLY DO HAVE (mentally, which is the realm of all TRUE CAUSATION) your desire right now. Once you really get into the FEELING that what you want already IS yours (mentally) you will SOON realize how quickly it grows into actual FORM. Keep out of your mind all fear-habits of thought. Know that fear-habits can be readily changed into FAITH-HABITS. Fear and faith are the same, one being one end of the stick and the other the other end of the same stick. The fear-end of the stick is a SHOVEL and will surely dig the grave of success; the FAITH-end is a JEWELLED CROWN ready to adorn the head of any who will wear it.

4. If necessary, COMPEL yourself to implicitly believe that the same Power that give you your desire in the beginning will also GIVE YOU THE WAYS AND MEANS OF ITS TRIUMPHANT FULFILLMENT.

5. Meditate carefully at frequent intervals on the REAL PURPOSE of your desire. This REAL PURPOSE of the desire, or the thing, is the ALL-IMPORTANT SPIRITUAL PROTOTYPE for the thing you want.

Also go over the Lord's Prayer very carefully several times daily, it will help you much in meditating more profoundly, and will TUNE YOUR MIND IN WITH THE POWER (GOD).

6. Every night before going to sleep, and every morning upon first awakening, make a solemn vow to live CLOSE to your God every conscious hour, to see only good in all, to entertain only good and constructive thoughts about everything and everyone.

7. Frequently mentally see yourself ALREADY ENJOYING YOUR FULFILLED DESIRE. Do this every time you think of the desire; and especially at night and morning, just before sleeping and at once upon awakening, for at these periods the subconscious element of mind is especially amenable to suggestions. In this way you DO ALREADY HAVE your desire perfectly fulfilled (mentally); and if you persist in it you shall surely have it soon in its physical form right in the midst of your life. For example, the great bridge that now spans the Golden Gate at San Francisco was first pictured COMPLETED and IN USE by many in the MIND of its designer before it became an actual reality. But by mentally picturing the bridge as ALREADY COMPLETED and SERVING MANY PEOPLE WELL the designer DREW from the WHOLE UNIVERSE the power necessary to have it actually built.

These SEVEN points are the keys, or steps, to the attainment of real success in any line of endeavor, MARK THEM WELL, and above all other things USE THEM! They are TRUTH! THEY WORK!

8

Instantaneous Healing

MASTER: It seems strange to one who has made real progress along God's great highway of Truth just how many mortals who are on the same journey will make detours that are altogether unnecessary, or will even turn and go in the opposite direction from their desired goal. For example, nearly everyone, it seems, is very much interested in a newly discovered disease, or in just disease as such, while the thing that all of us wish to know most about is PERFECT HEALTH and how to reach that rich experience that is spoken of in the Apocrypha, Ecc. 30:15-16, which reads: "Health and a good estate of body are above all gold: and a strong body above infinite wealth!" Of course we all know that it is impossible to find the Truth about HEALTH by holding our interest and attention on disease.

PUPIL: But we know that there is disease. Must we not reckon with this fact?

MASTER: One who recognizes disease as a reality has thus made his own law about it, and for him disease is inevitable. If disease is what you think and believe then disease is a fact for you. All bodily inharmony is first a thought and a belief; consequently its CURE is from the mental side also. It has been said that "the Absolute (Spirit) is like the air which carries odors, both good and bad, but which remains forever untainted by them." In the Absolute all is health and harmony; it may carry the beliefs of mortals in disease about with it yet it is never tainted by them!

PUPIL: But since the belief in disease is so widely prevalent is it not well for us to know how to handle disease, or belief in disease, from the spiritual standpoint?

MASTER: It would be more scientific to know how to handle HEALTH; and we shall devote this lesson to Healing, to living in conscious harmony with Life's laws. We shall start with the fine art of giving an effective spiritual treatment, or mental treatment. There are a number of most important points for the healer, or practitioner, to always remember and always practice in this respect.

PUPIL: Which point is the most important of them all?

MASTER: That is difficult to answer since all of them are vitally important; but one of them is this: The practitioner should have firmly fixed in mind the FACT that there is but ONE MIND and but ONE EXPRESSION of this one Mind although it fills all space with its numberless manifestations. This awareness removes the line of demarcation between patient and healer. Another vital essential is this: If one hopes to be of any help to a patient one must NOT give treatment for disease. That would surely INTENSIFY the disease! In giving a spiritual treatment the practitioner should utterly dismiss all thoughts of disease and of personality from the mind. To hold the thought on disease would mean MORE disease. Rather the healer should mentally see Life WHOLE,

FREE, AT PEACE and IN HARMONY through the power of the Radiant Christ within.

PUPIL: But suppose the patient is right there in front of you at the time of the treatment, that he is ill and in great pain. How can the practitioner avoid seeing the ill condition?

MASTER: If one is not sufficiently disciplined in mind to see through, or beyond, the condition one should not attempt to be a healer; or else such a one should confine his efforts exclusively to absent mental treatments. To see, or to believe in, any condition that a patient may seem to have disarms a practitioner immediately and renders his efforts impotent in behalf of the patient.

PUPIL: Are the absent mental treatments always just as effective as ones given face to face? Does not the distance of the patient from the source of treatment raise a barrier to the effectiveness of the treatments?

MASTER: A well trained and experienced practitioner is able to treat just as effectively absently as presently; and there are some who do better work absently. In Spirit there is neither TIME nor SPACE, and the distance of the patient from the healer makes no difference at all. You see the first mental step that the practitioner takes is that of clearing his or her mind of the presence of anything except the ONE GOD-SPIRIT. Thought is unbelievably fast in its transmission and can span the earth instantly; and it does not lose any of its power in the transmission! In giving an absent treatment the healer should be POSITIVE that the thought sent forth reaches the recipient NOW and with INFINITE POWER.

PUPIL: Why is it so vitally important to know that the Truth for the patient is his now? If he is ill it does not seem quite reasonable to me that he could be made whole right now.

MASTER: Nevertheless it is either now or never! In the Absolute the ONLY time there is the ETERNAL NOW. To it there is no past; nor is there any future. To it there is ONLY the PRESENT. If the practitioner holds the thought that the patient "will be all right," it will always be "will be" for the patient because the healer is POSTPONING the healing until some future time, and there is no future known to the Spirit, as I have said. Did Jesus ever say to any of those who were healed by Him: "You will be healed. Arise and go"? No, not ever. Always He spoke to them in the PRESENT tense; always He told them something to this effect: "You ARE WHOLE! Go in Peace!"

PUPIL: Just what are the mechanics of giving a mental treatment for one who is present personally with the practitioner?

MASTER: The steps in giving a successful treatment under such circumstances are these:

1. Have the patient RELAX physically as completely as possible, all over, toes, ankles, knees, spine, shoulders, arms, hands and even the eye-lids (for the eyes should be closed in the silence). The whole body of the patient should be as limp as possible. The greater the physical relaxation you may induce on the part of the patient the greater his RECEPTIVITY to the mental treatment will be.

2. Have the patient "empty" his conscious mind as completely as is possible, trying to think of nothing at all insofar as this can be done; have him try to make a vacuum of his mind, as it were. This complete RELAXATION of the conscious mind also induces a much greater RECEPTIVITY.

The healer MUST completely remove the line of demarcation between the patient and self. There are not two persons present, not really, not patient and practitioner. The two are ONE, and the establishment of this FACT firmly in the mind of the healer is of untold importance. REMEMBER that Mrs. Jones, practitioner, is NOT giving Mrs. Smith, patient, a mental treatment. As long as the one treating is aware of any sense of separation, or distinction, between patient and self there will be little if any results achieved.

3. Once all sense of separation is really removed from the practitioner's consciousness, the actual treatment is given. The patient is now in a passive, or receptive attitude, both mentally and physically. The healer is in an active, or generating, position. Yet the "two" are one, the one person being the negative pole, the other the positive, and between them the healing current of Life may now freely pass.

4. Into the Absolute the practitioner now projects a steady stream of positive, constructive, powerful thought-energy, at the beginning of which process the patient's name is either silently or audibly called in order that the flow of Spirit may be given DEFINITE DIRECTION. The receptive attitude of the patient picks up the flow of power and so it is made his own. The affirmation the healer uses at the beginning of the silence may be said aloud once or twice although this is not necessary. Into the Bosom of the Spirit, into the Fruitful Silence, the practitioner thinks and dwells with intense concentration and feeling, yet without any sense of strain whatsoever.

PUPIL: Upon what thought does the healer dwell in the silence?

MASTER: Upon the SPIRITUAL PROTOTYPE for the organ that may seem to be diseased, or for the thing or condition that may be desired. This SPIRITUAL PROTOTYPE is yet another thing that is of VITAL importance. To dwell in thought upon anything physical, anything which has form, is to be on the plane of LIMITATION, of SECONDARY CAUSATION, of EFFECT. BUT to think steadily upon the SPIRITUAL PROTOTYPE is to MENTALLY BE in the realm of the ABSOLUTE which is the INFINITE, which is FIRST CAUSE or PRIMARY CAUSATION, which is the CAUSE ITSELF and NOT the effect.

PUPIL: To me this spiritual prototype, important though I am sure it is, is the hardest thing in all of this study "to get hold of" mentally, the most difficult point to really understand. May I have some helpful pointers on this matter?

MASTER: That is true of many, in fact for nearly all "beginners" in this study. Perhaps the spiritual prototype is difficult for you because it is FORMLESS, Then, too, it may seem hard to understand because it is a new idea to you, one with which you are unfamiliar, of which you are not accustomed to thinking. Yet it is quite SIMPLE, once you know its nature. Here are some good rules to follow in this matter:

1. The spiritual prototype of anything is the thing itself in its most incipient state, is the actual origin of the thing in the Universal Mind.

2. To find the spiritual prototype for anything it is only necessary to determine in your own mind the PURPOSE of the thing, whatever it may be. This is an INFALLIBLE rule. Suppose, for example, one wished a good automobile and would like to know the spiritual prototype for it. One would mentally ask: "Exactly what is the PURPOSE of an automobile? What is it for? What does it do? What do I really want with a car" The automobile is, of course, an instrument, a means of PROGRESS, of rapid, pleasant, harmonious PROGRESS. This being so, then the spiritual prototype for an automobile is PROGRESS. At least this is what a car means to me; but in selecting a spiritual prototype for anything each one should think out for himself just what the PURPOSE of the thing is TO YOU.

PUPIL: Will you please give us a few other prototypes, and show us how they are arrived at? With still a few more examples to serve as guides, I am sure that I shall then know how to form my own prototypes for any particular thing desired or required.

MASTER: Very well; here are a few more. Let us take the head, for example, supposing that one had a belief in a violent headache. The head is the house of the brain; and the brain is the instrument of the mind, but in no sense the mind itself. What is the purpose of the mind? It is TO KNOW, TO KNOW GOD, the CAPACITY TO KNOW GOD! Can a CAPACITY TO KNOW ever really ache, or hurt, it being a FORMLESS THING? No it can not! The spiritual prototype for the head then, as I see it, is the CAPACITY TO KNOW GOD. Now for a minute let us consider the eyes. What is the purpose of the physical eye? It is the instrument of DISCERNMENT, which is a purely spiritual factor, DISCERNMENT as such having no form of its own. The CAPACITY OF DISCERNMENT is the spiritual prototype for the eyes, to me. Here are a few other spiritual prototypes for you; and in these that now follow I shall not explain for you just how I arrived at the conclusion. I shall name the particular organ, or part, of the body and the prototype for it, as I see it, and give you the benefit of thinking out for yourself just why I have chosen this particular prototype for each specific thing.

TEETH -Capacity to analyze and dissect God's ideas;

LUNGS -Capacity to KNOW LIFE as LIFE;

HEART -Capacity of LOVE;

STOMACH -Capacity of UNDERSTANDING;

LIVER -Capacity of FAITH;

KIDNEYS -Capacity of PURITY and CLEANLINESS.

The spiritual prototype, please remember always, is the purpose of the thing. Every physical thing has a purpose; consequently it has a SPIRITUAL CORRESPONDENCE. By letting your thoughts dwell upon the purpose of any physical organ, or thing, you make direct and most powerful CONTACT with the SOURCE OF ALL THINGS, with the FIRST CAUSE which projected forth from itself all concentrated things; for as Troward told me, "MATTER IS ONLY SPIRIT SLOWED DOWN TO A POINT OF VISIBILITY."

PUPIL: These examples will help me very much, I am sure. But now I am wondering just what is the best way to help ourselves, and others, forget human weaknesses, aches and pains, etc. It seems to me that most of us have the habit of dwelling too much in thought upon such negative things.

MASTER: I find that the very best way to get away from negative thoughts and feelings is this: TO DELIBERATELY TRAIN THE THOUGHT AND FEELING TO TRAVEL ALONG THE ROAD OF OUR BLESSINGS! Our every conscious moment DOES HAVE a blessing in it, if only one will look carefully for it, recognize it and be happy because of it. In looking for our blessings it will help greatly to recall to mind the many joys we have experienced, as well as those we hope to experience. In these ways we are able to forget the negative things of which the human side of us is so prone to accuse us.

PUPIL: May we have an illustration of this point, please? Something out of your own experience?

MASTER: Yes. Here is an actual experience in which I had a part. In Los Angeles several years ago a lady came to me with the problem of cancer, with which inharmony she had been told that she was grievously afflicted. Her whole attention, it seemed to me, was rigidly held on the limitation the cancerous condition was causing her, or should soon cause her to know. She owned and operated a restaurant, and was doing much of the work herself. Several doctors, she said, had told her there was no cure for her, that the disease had spread until an operation was not to be considered, that she must stay off her feet and spend most of her time, such as remained to her, in bed, etc. This, she said, meant that she must go out of business, of course, and when she did that she would be in dire want, in fact an object of charity. With her mind filled with these negative thoughts of illness and lack, which were certain to come unless she could be healed, she came to see me.

When I had talked the matter over with her I asked her to let me think things over for three days before giving her my decision about accepting her case for mental treatment. I asked for this delay in order that I might thoroughly check to see how much time I could allot to her, to see if I could arrange for all the time she would require. After two days of changing some appointments, and postponing some others which were not really urgent, I told the lady to come. My first question to her was this:

"Do you absolutely BELIEVE what Jesus told His disciples, as recorded in Mark 10:27, and which reads as follows: 'With man it is impossible, but not with God; FOR WITH GOD ALL THINGS ARE POSSIBLE!' ?"

She assured me positively that she DID BELIEVE just that; but said that she found her own mind too untrained and chaotic to keep her thought and feeling OFF what seemed to be the inevitable and hold it ON THE FACT that God IS the ONLY POWER there is, that HE is FOREVER PRESENT, ALWAYS AMENABLE TO SUGGESTION, ETERNALLY RESPONSIVE AND ALWAYS CREATIVE. Hence she wished the help of the Spirit through me.

I told her that I should ask her to know with me HOURLY, continually, that her relation to God is always I-AM, and that whenever she thought or said "I-AM" to remember that she was thinking or saying, in reality, "GOD IS." I told her also that God created her out of Himself, for Himself, and that to Him and in Him she was forever complete, whole, perfect. "God is love!" I told her; and I asked her to always try to feel His Great Love surging through her. I quoted I John 4:16-18 to her: "God is love; and he that DWELLETH IN LOVE DWELLETH IN GOD and GOD IN HIM!" I also asked her to know that God is LIFE, Intelligent, Loving, Harmonious, Creative Life, and asked her to HOLD HER CONSCIOUS THOUGHT AND FEELING on these things.

"But," she protested, "you have not given me any affirmation for MY cancer!"

"Did you say 'My cancer'?" I asked her with much feeling and emphasis. "Do you really want cancer, my dear? Are you determined to have it? If not, then why ARE YOU CLAIMING IT FOR YOUR OWN by saying 'my cancer'? Remember thoughts are things!"

"Oh, no!" she exclaimed. "I see what you mean. Just listen to me. I must conquer this negative habit of thought."

I assured her yet again that she WAS a Divine Child, that all of her needs were forever supplied THROUGH HER RECOGNITION of them. I then told her to try to constantly keep in her consciousness thoughts which contained some quality of the following:

Belief Confidence Conviction Credit Honesty Patience Reliance Sincerity .and other ideas in which there was some of the ESSENCE OF FAITH. I stressed the fact that by keeping these things in mind her THOUGHT and FEELING would have the ESSENCE of FAITH in them; and that she should soon form the HABIT of thinking in that way. It was my endeavor to get her to keep her mind OFF HERSELF and ON THE THINGS OF THE SPIRIT. I knew that if I could get her to do this HABITUALLY God should take care of the rest of the matter.

This lady assured me that she would try to do exactly as I had asked although it seemed more plausible to doubt than to believe that she could be in perfect health again after so much suffering, and the opinions of several doctors that she was doomed.

Still again I told her most positively that it is written: "GOD IS WITH YOU TO SAVE YOU!" I asked her to remember that FAITH IS ALIVE and that it LEADS TO MORE LIFE which doubt is dead and leads nowhere. The leading characteristic of faith is that it constantly flows and burns with constantly increasing brightness and expectancy. Faith always travels in the one direction of understanding. Doubt is a blight upon every effort towards Truth.

This patient came to see me regularly every day for some two weeks; and her condition began to improve from the very start. Then she had only absent treatment at frequent intervals, with an occasional visit in person, for another six weeks. At the end of two months she was entirely free from any evidences of cancer, free in body, in mind and in affairs. Immediately she began to build up physically and when I last saw her, some two of three years after she first came to me, she was in robust health, prospering in business and sure of her contact with the Spirit.

PUPIL: This illustration clears up in my mind, when I go back over it point by point, a number of ideas which were very hazy and uncertain to me. Thank you. I do know that doubts make one wretched from morning until night.

MASTER: Exactly so. And it would seem that after a while people who indulge in them would learn this fact and make an "about face" and a "forward march" in the direction of faith. Faith is a brightly glowing light and lives within us. It has its source in the fountain-head of INTUITION. Its radiance is seen in the long shafts of splendor that lead one forever upward into the kingdom of the beautiful, the true, and the good.

PUPIL: If one does not have any faith, how does one get it?

MASTER: One does NOT get faith. EVERY SOUL ALREADY HAS IT! It has been yours forever; it is as much a part of you, of your Divine Being, as is your heart, your lungs, your mind: It is a gift as precious as Life itself, and is born of Life itself, forever innate in every living soul. It is true that some are less aware of faith than others through having neglected it, through having blighted it with doubts, fears, anxiety, etc. But the quality IS still there, and by cultivation it will spring into fullness again. All that is required is this: THAT YOU EXERCISE THE FAITH THAT YOU ALREADY HAVE for just a few weeks. Deliberately look for it! Insist on seeing it! PERSIST IN USING IT!

9

Is Desire A Divine Impulse?

MASTER: Is desire a Divine Impulse? One hears this question asked in as many different forms, it seems, as there are humans. So frequently is it propounded and discussed it seems to me that it will be helpful to answer it from Troward's standpoint; after you have studied and meditated upon it from his views you will arrive at your own satisfactory conclusion.

PUPIL: I am glad that you have brought this up for us. I have often wished I knew just what God wanted me to do when I have been undecided about some move, perhaps a momentous decision.

MASTER: The only way anyone can fully understand Life's law of attraction is through seeing what it does under certain given conditions. In a tree it is growth; in an animal it is development; in all of nature it is evolution. From the lowest to the highest forms all growth is prompted by the organized creature pushing forth in its own accomplishment. One can not do otherwise than believe in the law of unfoldment which is the hallowed desire of the All-Originating Life to see ITSELF more and more fully manifested. Since we as humans are branches of the one and only tree of Life this fact is also true of us.

PUPIL: May I ask a question, please?

MASTER: Certainly, any time.

PUPIL: Do you mean that all growth is a result of a DESIRE for self-expression, that all evolution is within the great Creative Mind?

MASTER: Just so; and each of us is a direct result of that desire. Therefore we should learn to TRUST OUR DESIRES! There is but the ONE GREAT DESIRE and practically all of our individual desires are reflections of that one. Man's desire, his REAL desire, is for GOOD. No rational person would desire anything else for himself or another.

PUPIL: But many philosophies teach that we must conquer, must overcome, must rise above all desire in order to be perfected. How do you answer this?

MASTER: I stand fast in what has already been said herein. I hold fast to the firm conviction that our desires ARE DIVINE IMPULSES which stimulate us to GROWTH and CONSTANT DEVELOPMENT. Without desires we should be mere automatons, should have no wish to progress and grow. It is impossible for one to crush out all desires without RUINING self, spirituality, physically, morally and mentally. The desires, the longings, we have are STIMULI, are URGES for EXPRESSION, from the holy citadel of God within ourselves!

PUPIL: Is it true then that if we would draw into us any particular benefit we have only to impress the desire for it firmly upon the subconscious phase of mind and hold it unwaveringly? Should we do this just as an impression of sound is made upon a phonograph disk before being reproduced? Should we do this knowing that said desire is instantly transmitted into the One Great

Creative Energy which is always responsive, and that is sure to be manifested in our own physical world?

MASTER: That is just what I mean. Let me give you another illustration. I know a very fine and very wise lady in Los Angles who after returning from marketing found that she had misplaced her car keys; and she had an urgent appointment awaiting her downtown within a little while. She had taken her groceries from the car into the kitchen. After looking around for the keys in every place that she could logically think of she had still failed to find them. So she told herself (her subconscious phase of mind); "I want those car keys. I must have them. Now where are they? YOU KNOW!" Almost immediately she had the desire to empty the bag of potatoes into the kitchen sink. But she ridiculed that idea, and repeated her desire to find the keys. She did this two or three times, meanwhile keeping up her search for the keys; and every time she received back the feeling that she should empty the potato-bag. It was her habit to let her maid empty the bags and put the purchases away; and the idea of emptying the potato-bag seemed foolish anyway. But the impulse remained urgently with her although she could not see how her car keys could possibly be in the potato-bag. So she did empty the bag into the sink and almost instantly she heard a metallic sound. She looked and, behold, there were the missing keys!

PUPIL: Her deep desire to find the keys brought her the answer? It seems very simple.

MASTER: And it IS very simple once you know the responsiveness of the law of subjective mind. This lady knew that law.

PUPIL: If she really knew the law why did she not recognize the answer to her desires the very first time she was impressed to empty the potato-bag?

MASTER: The lady to whom I refer is a very highly-educated woman, a keen student of logic. While she truly does believe in the intuitive power of the mind to capture an idea from the Infinite the old race-habit of giving REASON first place had not been entirely uprooted from her consciousness. When intuition told her plainly to empty the bag reason set up an argument and told her that the impulse was foolish. The controversy between reason and intuition continued within her for several minutes. Then because of her study of Truth, and her application of it, she was reminded that INTUITION, and not logic, IS THE TRUE KEY OF LIFE! So she was impelled to do as she was bidden. When she did so her desire had fulfillment as its correlative. Always DESIRE and FULFILLMENT are bound together as CAUSE and EFFECT through the universal law of attraction!

PUPIL: It still seems to me that a true student of Truth should have thoughts, feelings and desires so trained in the right direction that logic could not go wrong in its conclusions.

MASTER: One does not change life-long habits of reasoning overnight. Like everything else, complete change is a matter of growth. The fact that she did obey the still small voice within, and that thus was her problem solved, are all that really mattered. In time this lady, like all of us, will learn to instantly recognize the voice of intuition when it speaks and will no longer question, nor reason, will ONLY OBEY. When we all reach that point, as we can and shall through faithful study and practice, there will be NO PROBLEM IN ALL OF HUMAN EXPERIENCE THAT WILL FAIL TO YIELD ITS ANSWER!

There is a lot of truth in the old saying: "Take care of the heart and the head will take care of itself."

PUPIL: But is not the road to the attainment of true wisdom a long, hard one?

MASTER: It is long alright, being Infinite in scope; but it is NOT hard. It is like the story of the two men who are walking to Rome. One asked the other why he had chosen a road that was so full of stones. His companion replied that he had not been aware of any stones in the road, and suggested that they sit down by the roadside and take off their shoes. This they did; and the one who had been complaining found a PEBBLE IN HIS SHOE. But there was nothing wrong with the road itself.

PUPIL: The road is then what each one makes of it for himself? Is that your idea?

MASTER: That is right. The broad highway of Truth is in fact, to me at least, the most interesting road in all of life. It takes times and interesting, happy effort to establish an unbroken consciousness of the PERFECT RECIPROCAL ACTION between the desire for expression as it exists in the Creative Energy and in the individual mind. It is true that by RIGHTLY ESTABLISHING our relation to the Great Parent Mind we can gradually grow into any condition that we may desire, provided of course that we first make of ourselves, through our habitual mental attitude, the PERSON WHO CORRESPONDS to those conditions. One can never get away from the Law of Correspondences. This SCIENCE of Correspondence, or of CAUSE and EFFECT, is as infallible as is mathematics; and as in mathematics its principles must be mastered before one can habitual feel: "My Father and I are ONE!" Yes, our DESIRES are our own IMMORTAL SELVES SEEKING FULLER EXPRESSION; and one may soon prove to the doubting, bewildered self that one CAN ABSOLUTELY TRUST THE DESIRES.

PUPIL: Somehow it is still a little difficult for me to accept the feeling that my desires are Divine impulses, or the Divine Nature Itself seeking expression through me. It seems to me that desire is selfish and often wrong, even bad for one.

MASTER: Did not Jesus say; "Seek and ye shall find!" Just why would anybody seek a thing?

PUPIL: Because he wanted that for which he was seeking.

MASTER: Very good. Are not wants and DESIRES the same? Jesus also said: "ASK believing that you have and ye shall have!" Why would one ask for a thing?

PUPIL: Because he desires it and feels it would be good for him.

MASTER: Correct. Yet again the Master said: "Except ye become as a little child ye shall in no wise enter the kingdom of heaven." If one desires to grow into the NEW LIFE OF LIBERTY and JOY, indeed one must become as a little child.

PUPIL: And just what did Jesus mean by that?

MASTER: Just what He said. Observe a child, any child, rich or poor. Its very impulse is desire, is to want something. All children are simply one continual incarnation of "gimme" and "want to." Naturally the child's wants are but the forerunner of the man and his wants; and in the adult desires are as natural as in the child.

PUPIL: This desire idea is truly a new one to me. But I like it.

MASTER: You will learn to love and trust your desires as your spiritual understanding expands. Vitality, which is Life, is born of desire, is the child of Love. You will be amazed at the rapid progress you will make once you have really made up your own mind to trust your desires. The more you learn to trust your wants the greater will be your flow of faith.

PUPIL: But must there not be a check somewhere on desires? A sorting of the good and the bad? All desires are not holy, are they?

MASTER: One must be rational, of course. Troward writes in his "Edinburgh Lectures" that "there is nothing wrong with the evidences of a HEALTHY MIND in a HEALTHY BODY." This study presupposes that a sincere student of Truth will not harbor evil desires, that his or her mentality is normal, the behavior normal. This being so the desires of such a one should also be only natural, rational, good; and if this is so then the desires of that one are Divine impulses. Let me suggest that you read the personal letter that Troward wrote to me, an exact copy of which is found in my book, "Attaining Your Desires". Then you will see yet more clearly why you should TRUST YOUR DESIRES, recognizing as you do that DESIRES ARE DIVINE IMPULSES!

9

Supreme Self-Freedom

PUPIL: So, SUPREME SELF-FREEDOM is our very wonderful subject for today, is it? I am sure that you shall prove to us that supreme self-freedom can be ours, that MIND DOES RULE THE WORLD.

MASTER: You may always be quite certain that YOUR MIND RULES YOUR WORLD; and you may always know that your individual world is a branch of the Universal World. Your mind makes of your world a thing of BEAUTY, PEACE and ABSOLUTE FREEDOM, if only you so will.

PUPIL: I am convinced that this is true IF only one could truly control one's mind, thoughts and feelings at all times. I know that others have attained this mastery, this self-control; but somehow it does not seem to be for me, as much as I desire it.

MASTER: At one time in our lives each of us thought this same thing about the multiplication-tables. How difficult they seemed to us as children; yet each of us mastered them by PERSISTENT EFFORT. It is like that with ABSOLUTE SELFFREEDOM. It is dormant within each soul, waiting only for us to call upon it, to arouse it, to recognize it, to give it our attention, our concentrated observation, in our every thought, our every feeling, every act. It is not difficult to have if we make it FIRST in our lives just as a great scientist puts his science BEFORE EVERYTHING ELSE! In theory at least all of us realize that we get only what we REACH FOR and REACH FOR STEADILY.

PUPIL: Is not Annette Kellerman, the great swimmer, an example of this? Was she not a cripple as a child, and considered hopelessly crippled?

MASTER: Yes, she was. But through insistent, persistent, determined, steady effort she became the physically-perfect woman, a model for the women of the world. Her science was the science of health, the science of physical beauty and perfection. There are many sciences; and each of us may select the one with which we are most in tune and pursue it to a dazzling goal.

PUPIL: But has not science boasted that it has Disproved the Holy Bible?

MASTER: It may be that some scientists make this boast. But it is not true. The fact of the matter is that SCIENCE HAS CONFIRMED THE TRUTH OF THE BIBLE! It might be said that science has written a new Bible for the THINKING mind merely by clarifying the old one. Science has made of the Bible the Book supreme for those who are determined to live HERE and NOW. Science has proved that "THE WORD" of Life, of the Spirit, IS A LIVING WORD OF POWER! Truly "the heavens do declare the glory of God, and the firmament sheweth His handiwork."

In reading your Bible always substitute the word "Subconscious Mind" for the word "Lord." Try this faithfully for awhile and see what an astonishing growth you will make. Try this with such passages as Isaiah 40:31, Mark 29:30, Luke 18:29-30 and a host of others. Look about you; look at the results achieved by those who have learned to LOVE, to USE and to TRUST the MIND. Strength, power, beauty, television, wire-photography, microscope, telescope, spectroscope, all of these, yes ALL of ALL THINGS, are RESULTS from the Great Creative Energy whose progress, harmony; telephone, wireless, airplanes, chief attributes are these:

1. It is EVER-PRESENT, EVERYWHERE;
2. It is always AMENABLE to suggestion;
3. It is FOREVER RESPONSIVE;
4. It is ETERNALLY CREATIVE.

This God-ENERGY, REMEMBER, manifests in the MIND OF MAN, in fact IS the mind of man. The three Bible-references given above, and many others, teach us that if one puts the DEVELOPMENT of the DIVINE SPARK WITHIN FIRST, over all else, the DIVINE in return will make that one FIRST with it! Truly then the BEST Life has to give is the possession of that one!

PUPIL: Am I right in believing that the precious promises of the Bible all hinge upon our making intelligent decisions, Loving Life (God) FIRST in everything? And if I do is EVERYTHING I may desire sure to be mine?

MASTER: That is right, IF YOU MAKE GOD FIRST, if you really DO make Him FIRST. That is to say we should make it our FIRST effort to KNOW LIFE'S LAWS and TO LIVE THEM! In this connection please read over and over again, or better still MEMORIZE letter perfect, the 22nd Chapter of Job, beginning at verse 21 and continuing to the end of the Chapter. The promises given there, the power, the freedom, the plenty, ARE yours, exactly as promised, if you will take the time, the effort, to become ACQUAINTED with the LOVING PARENT-POWER which is always ABLE, and ever MORE THAN WILLING to do these things IN YOU, THROUGH YOU. As you read be sure to bear in mind constantly that the 21st verse is the KEY to all of the others that follow it. The gist of this whole passage in Job is this: WE GET OUT OF LIFE EXACTLY WHAT WE PUT INTO IT, PLUS MUCH INCREASE AS INTEREST ON OUR FAITH! Some state this in a more homely way by saying that "we get what we pay for, and no more."

PUPIL: I have often wondered about this in connection with tithing. Is it true that tithing is a very old Law which has the greatest power back of it?

MASTER: Indeed tithing IS A LAW which has MUCH POWER in it! I have tithed for twenty-five years, religiously so. The practice of tithing is a divine-habit-forming virtue. People tithe because they recognize God and wish to DEVELOP their recognition and expectancy. Regular, systematic tithers are those who have formed the HABIT of COUNTING THEIR BLESSINGS. As a result their BLESSINGS CONSTANTLY INCREASE! Did not Abraham give a tenth of his ALL to Melchizedek as a TOKEN of acknowledgment that his SUCCESSES WERE FROM GOD? And when Jesus sent His disciples forth into the cities of Israel He expressly forbade them to take with them any money or provisions. Why? Because He wished the people of those cities to recognize God in His servants, and to support them with their tithes. As Saint Paul said: "The people who receive spiritual instruction shall administer some of their GOOD to him who gives the instruction." IT IS a FACT abundantly PROVED that the HABIT OF TITHING IS A SURE ROAD TO SUPREME SELF-FREEDOM!

PUPIL: Am I to understand that the habit of tithing would give me a consciousness of an ABIDING PARTNERSHIP WITH GOD?

Because my tithing is to God and His servants? Is this correct? Does one tithe to God's cause in recognition, in loving recognition, of Divine guidance? Does one necessarily have to tithe to churches only?

MASTER: No, one need not tithe to churches only. Some people tithe regularly to missionary organizations, some to charities, and many tithe to individuals who work in God's vineyards, irrespective of organizations or affiliations. The value of tithing lies in the ESTABLISHMENT OF THE FEELING OF CONSTANT DIVINE PARTNERSHIP. Tithing brings one into the HIGH and FRUITFUL CONSCIOUSNESS of GOD AND COMPANY, UNlimited! If one keeps in CONSCIOUS touch with the Ever-Present, Responsive Substance of Life by regularly returning to it some of the substance (funds) which it has placed in his stewardship, this constitutes a practical acknowledgment of blessings and thus INCREASES THE BLESSINGS MANYFOLD. The ancient Israelites PROVED this fact consistently; and for centuries the Jews have practiced tithing, as they do today. The Mormons of today prove this Law constantly also. When I was lecturing in Salt Lake City during the "Depression" there was not a SINGLE MORMON, or MORMON FAMILY ON RELIEF! The reason is obvious. THEY TITHE!

PUPIL: I did not realize that tithing was so very great a stimulant for the steady inflow of supply; but now it seems to me that it would give one the same sense of security one has when the taxes are paid in full.

MASTER: That is right. After all your money is yourself; You are God's, your money is His also. Humanity exchanges its abilities, integrity, labor, etc., for money. In my thirty-five years as a practitioner I have had thousands of people come to me for spiritual help for increased supply; BUT in all of that time I have NEVER HAD A SOLITARY TITHER seek my help for financial increase! In fact I have had very few tithers, ones who religiously follow the practice, ever seek my help for ANY KIND OF INHARMONY! Tithing DOES carry with it a WEALTH OF BLESSINGS. GIVING IS WORSHIP! If one REALLY worships God, and considers Him one's BEST business partner, one acknowledges His help by giving to His cause FIRST. The average person gives a mere pittance to God, AFTER they have paid everything else. That is NOT tithing in any sense. A tithe is not a tithe unless it is ten percent. The tithe should be paid first, from the gross profit; and it should be tendered in genuine love, thanksgiving and joy, if not in sheer abandon.

PUPIL: Is tithing required by the Intelligent, Creative Power in Life? Surely God does not need the money, or lands, or cattle.

MASTER: Tithing is voluntary. Yet it IS REQUIRED if one wishes a continual increase of blessings. It is a great joy to recognize God as a partner.

To me a partner means one of whom we are fond, with whom we labor for a common good, and with whom we happily SHARE in love. In order to receive benefits from tithing there MUST be JOY IN GIVING. To tithe grudgingly yields no blessings, or few at best. "He who gives HIMSELF with his gifts feeds three, himself, his hungering neighbor and ME!" Tithing brings with it an ABIDING SENSE OF SECURITY, has within its loving bosom an abundance of SUCCESS-IDEAS which when adopted bring health, wealth and happiness. This is the LAW OF TITHING.

PUPIL: Thank you for this lesson on tithing. I should like to hear much more about it. But are you going to tell us today how to reason ourselves into certainty?

MASTER: This is hardly what I meant when we were discussing reasoning out an affirmation before trying to absorb it. For example let us consider freedom. Freedom is joy; joy is freedom. But it seems there are few who have either freedom or joy to any great extent. Many seem to be bound by miseries; their every day is full of discord. To them work, all kinds of work, is disagreeable. To them most people are unbearable; things that happen are awful. The weather is abominable; it rains when it shouldn't; when it should rain it doesn't. They buy things, then regret it. They sell things and then are hurt because they didn't receive more money. If they don't go places they feel slighted; if they do go places they feel sure they were snubbed. If they don't have things they are despondent; if they do have things they are not what they want, etc., etc., etc.

PUPIL: Heavens, is this the average person you are describing?

MASTER: No. I am just giving you an intimate glimpse of a person in bondage, of ones who have not trained their minds to HOLD ONLY THOUGHTS OF ABSOLUTE FREEDOM. Perfect joy and freedom are yours NOW. TAKE them and make them YOURS.

PUPIL: How may one enter upon these joy thoughts at will?

MASTER: That is the place for the affirmation. Take, for example, the thought: "THE VERY BEST LIFE HAS TO GIVE IS MINE NOW!" Reason about this for a minute. Why is it true? Because Life (God) made me out of Himself and LIVES IN ME. The very life of me is God. Life is happy; life is free; life is health; life is wealth; Life is ALL GOOD.

PUPIL: I can see this BUT suppose that when you have satisfied yourself this is true some member of the family, or some friend, jabs you with a very unkind remark? What then? Are you supposed to laugh that off?

MASTER: If you REALLY ARE CONSCIOUS that the BEST Life has to give is yours, you will instantly realize at all times that you are not supposed to try to live for another. You have all you can do to keep the stream of joy flowing through your own consciousness. When I first began my study with Troward he cautioned me every day: "Watch your THOUGHTS and FEELINGS! They DO TAKE FORM, you know!" And he really got that great Truth across to my consciousness. When I went to Ruan Manor to study with him, I had been accustomed to a personal maid all of my life. I took my maid with me when I went to Troward. There was not one modern convenience where I lived in Ruan Manor; and none could be obtained thereabouts. We had been there just a month when Marie came to me in tears and told me she was heartbroken to leave me but she could not stay in that awful place any longer; she just must go back to Paris. She was too lonely, etc. Of course my first thoughts were: "If Marie goes, what shall I do? Here we are miles from anywhere, with no conveniences of any kind.

What does this mean? Why should this disaster come to me now, of all times, when I really am trying to know God?" Just when my thoughts reached that station, and were gathering momentum, Troward's warning: "WATCH YOUR THOUGHTS!" came to my mind and I stopped right there. I began to use the will exercise he had taught me. I also used affirmations he had given me, to hold my thoughts where the Creative Power in THOUGHTS AND FEELINGS could produce what I wanted. What I wanted most was FREEDOM TO CONTINUE WITH MY STUDY. I deliberately held my thoughts in the RIGHT place.

Only two days later the lady from whom I rented our rooms came to me and said she believed that Marie had been trying to tell her that she was leaving me (Marie was French and spoke no English) and that she wished she could find me another good personal maid before she went to Paris. I told the lady this was the case. She said that her daughter was coming home from London in just a few days, that her daughter had worked there for several years as a good personal maid, and that she felt sure the girl would be happy to work for me in that capacity. Marie left after teaching the other girl just how I wished things done; and the new maid was as satisfactory as the first. In this episode I had my first good lesson in knowing that I must WATCH MY THOUGHTS, that THEY DO BECOME THINGS!

PUPIL: You have said that your favorite affirmation is the Lord's Prayer. Please show us how you would reason this out in order to better understand it before using it, part of it at least.

MASTER: Very well. The first two words of that prayer carry a tremendous power, if they are thought over, or spoken, with much feeling. What does "Our Father" suggest? Our Father, our very own Father? When you were a child what was your idea of your father? Your idea of him may have been exaggerated but you BELIEVED him to be rich beyond all words, influential, kind, loving, good, always ready to give, to help, to comfort, to make you happy and to see that you had everything that your little heart could desire. Then try to feel yourself as a child of God, with all the enthusiasm of a child. Know that you are so like HIM that He adores you, guides you, shields you, protects you, gives you everything He has to give in generous quantity, that you are, and that you have, HIS ALL.

Do this with the whole prayer. Think about it all, understand and assimilate it all; then USE IT ALL! If you will do your part you will find that the Father-Principle in life IS ALWAYS RESPONSIVE! Your objective quality of mind may not know what is best for you because it can only realize the objective and limited side of Life. But THE FATHER IN YOU, HE KNOWS! Ask Him, be guided by Him. Your real desires are but reflections from Him which shine through and register in your mind.

PUPIL: Would it not be a good idea for us to frequently refer back to the lesson on "Desire, a Divine Impulse" when there is any confusion of mind about desires?

MASTER: Yes, that is recommended; in fact I trust that you will frequently review all of the Lessons of this Course. And I devoutly wish that you would earnestly TRY to MAKE GOD FIRST in your heart, and mind, and soul, and daily and hourly life. If you will, it will mean for you a life of SUPREME SELF-FREEDOM and truly you will MAKE OF YOURSELF a reflection of God's OWN IDEA who is the PERFECTED you. To this end I recommend the following, all of which I urge you to memorize, letter perfect. I also URGE you to USE and USE and yet again USE these points and affirmations, faithfully and regularly. Here they are:

For DAILY, Systematic, Loving Use:

Your hourly effort should be that of fully realizing your true place in the Great Plan of Life.

Just what is this TRUE place for each individual? It is, as Troward taught me, the following three things:

WORSHIP of God Alone;

The absolute EQUALITY of all individuals;

Complete CONTROL of all else.

Affirmations:

I AM intelligent, Loving Spirit, LIVING in Creative Love and Power!

In Him do I LIVE and MOVE and have my WHOLE BEING!

I AM a specialized PART OF God's own Self-Manifestation! God IS specialized in me; therefore I AM perfect Harmony!

I AM direct knowledge of ALL Truth! I AM perfect Intuition! I AM Spiritual perception at its fullness! There is but ONE Wisdom; therefore I AM Perfect Wisdom!

My mind IS a center of DIVINE operation; therefore I AM always thinking good thoughts, speaking only constructive words! Time is Eternal; God is the ONLY Giver! His Loving Intelligence is continually working IN and THROUGH me; hence I AM ever working correctly. I AM thinking the RIGHT thoughts, in the RIGHT way, at the RIGHT time, towards the RIGHT result! God's work IN and THROUGH me is always WELL done!

I AM Specialized Spirit! I AM always receiving rich, powerful inspirations from the Great, Universal, Parent Spirit. Divine Intelligence is always thinking NEW, FRESH, CLEAR ideas through me, ones far beyond any I have ever known before. My prayers are the outflow of the Great Oversoul of the Universe. They go forth in His Name; and ALWAYS they ACCOMPLISH that for which I send them. GOD IS GLORIFYING HIMSELF IN AND THROUGH ME NOW!

10

Exercises For Health

1. Breathing, Bathing and Short, Easy, Profitable Exercises for Health:

Note: (These exercises are given as a stimulant to your capacity, both mental and physical. Mind and body are one. When both body and mind are strong happiness and success usually follow, especially if one adds to them mental and bodily efficiency.)

Correct breathing is one of Nature's most powerful methods of building a powerful body, a perfect body. Let us begin now to breathe correctly and profitably. If these exercises are taken as intended there will not be any strain. The first exercise is this:

Upon arising in the morning first drink two or three glasses of water. The effect will be better if you will take the water just as hot as you can bear to drink it, with the juice of one-half a lemon in it. Then stand erect, or else lie flat on the floor. Exhale completely. Whether standing or lying on floor bend knees slightly. As you exhale contract both the chest and the diaphragm, pushing the latter OUT and DOWN as far as possible without causing strain. Naturally this will extend the abdomen. Then without lifting your chest pull abdomen IN as far as you can. Then without any attempt at correct breathing push abdomen OUT and IN rapidly at least twelve times.

After you have mastered the above exercise for the abdomen and diaphragm, take the next exercise -for not more than two minutes each time. This exercise is: Stand erect, or lie flat on the back. Exhale completely, contracting chest. Then slowly inhale through the nostrils, trying not to allow chest to move. Let the diaphragm push the abdomen down, then hold the breath for three or four seconds. Exhale slowly. Then forget all about abdomen and diaphragm and inhale deeply, letting breath lift chest walls up and out to their fullest capacity. Hold breath a few seconds and exhale all the breath.

If you will practice these two simple exercises each morning for ten days, you will note a great improvement in physical condition and vitality, the head and mind will be clearer and you will have a real zest for work.

No doubt you know that the right kind of bath is a splendid nervetonic, as well as a most important point in attaining physical and mental perfection. When bathing for cleanliness the water should be of blood temperature, never hot or cold. After the cleansing bath, fill the wash-basin with cold water. Scoop up two handfuls and apply to the forehead, and rub up and down the face. Dip hands in cold water again and shake off all surplus water, then rub off balance behind the ears. Repeat process on back of neck. These things soothe and strengthen the nerves.

A certain way of relief for constipation is this: First, meditate on the perfect and harmonious action of Life. In Nature one does not find either inaction or over-action. Think over how the Life in your body regulates the flow of blood, the action of the muscles, both voluntary and involuntary, and how all of these things are done in perfect harmony. For a regulatory exercise in relieving constipation the following is splendid. First, as soon as you arise in the morning, drink two glasses of hot water. Then stand, or lie on the back on floor.

Breathe deeply. As you inhale extend the abdomen and contract it as you exhale, contracting it all you possibly can. Do this without letting chest rise at all. Do the exercise rapidly, vigorously, always inhaling through the nostrils and exhaling through the mouth. Take about eight seconds for each complete breath. Do this for a minute or two then use another minute to recover normal breathing. A second exercise is recommended; and it is better if taken in connection with the one just given. It is this: Again stand erect or lie on the back, preferably the latter. Draw first the right knee and then the left up to the chest as snug as possible.

Inhale deeply as you put foot down to floor and exhale as you draw knee down to chest. Do this exercise rapidly, vigorously for one minute. After the exercise try to get into the feeling of gratitude that you ARE able to CONSCIOUSLY tune in with the harmonious action of Life. If you keep thinking deeply on the fact that ALL of the qualities of Life must be present anywhere and everywhere that Life is, the feeling of ONE-ness will come and you will enjoy the thrill of it. The very best there is is yours now and the perfect movement is manifesting NOW.

How to Retain Youth and to Banish Gray Hairs and Wrinkles if They Offend You:

Think, know, feel, be thankful for the fact that Life as Life has NO age and yet is ageless. Give this fact a little profound thought every day. Soon you will get the deep and abiding awareness of it. In your mind's eye, and in memory, try to recall how you felt about certain things when you were twenty, how you looked then, and acted, and bubbled over with energy. Ask yourself if your point of view about Life in general has changed radically, or if you have simply forgotten how to Live Life and Love it, as you did then. The emotions, the fine understanding, the zest for activity, as you had them in youth have not glided off without leaving a trace in the development of your advancing years.

Try to give yourself a careful going over mentally each day, and LIVE for a while each day the experiences of your youth, bringing them back into your FEELING. Perhaps you say: "Oh, but youth is so foolish!" That may be so; but remember always that it DOES THINGS! Try to weed out and destroy the doubts of your advancing years; try to prune out of yourself, out of your thought and feeling, your tendency towards being over-conservative. Old age is only an OSSIFIED IDEA! Being over-conservative and opposed to progress and change are the things that make one old, and usually impotent. Your youth was all right; LIVE IT AGAIN! Live it in FEELING and keep the feeling bolstered temporarily by making mental pictures of your happy, cocksure self as you were at twenty. SEE your face, figure and hair as they were then.

And each day do the following exercise for the banishment of gray hair. Vigorously RUB the whole scalp, from the nape of the neck up over the crown to the hair-line on the forehead, using Glover's Mange Cure. This liquid is not for dogs only, but is also an excellent tonic and stimulant for human hair. Rub the liquid well into the scalp. The gray hair may fall out for a while after you have done this exercise faithfully for several days but keep it up and new hair will come in with the natural color of the hair of your youth. Yes, mentally go back to twenty and balance its vitality with your present wisdom! KNOW with all of your heart and soul, and all of your emotional self, that Life as Life IS manifesting in you in a particular way in order that it may find new avenues for expressing itself as the JOY of living.

Make an hourly effort to keep in your consciousness your JOYS only. MAKE THEM REGISTER! Deliberately BE HAPPY and your body will respond to it in every way. It will also help, particularly for the ladies, to sit in front of the vanity a half-hour each day, seeing yourself NOT as you are now (if aged) but AS YOU WERE in youth. Do this with deep concentration, deepest feeling, affirming something like this: "I AM Life. I AM YOUTH, eternal YOUTH!" The important thing, however, is to SEE yourself as youth, to FEEL youth, to know that you ARE youth. Soon you will find a decided improvement setting in. Thought IS always creative!

Soon you will look younger; soon you will feel younger; soon you will be younger, not in years of course but years do not make aging. Some are old at twenty-five; others are young at eighty. It is flexibility of mind, a keen enjoyment of living, that make for elasticity of muscle and for youth.

A Method of Attracting Money:

Meditate on the RICHES of Life as it really is. All that we can see or think of in Nature shows us only ABUNDANCE. Every growing thing is amply provided for. The grass and trees, and other growing things, do not know poverty. In the soil, in the air, in the sunshine, there is an abundance of nourishment for all. THINK about this great fundamental Truth because it applies to YOU also. Wherever you may be, whatever your station in life may be, the Creator of all Life HAS just as amply provided for you as He has for the grass, the birds, all of Nature. It is not His fault that all do not express or manifest this bounty; people are as poor, or will soon be as rich, as they ACCEPT for themselves in the CONSCIOUSNESS. Everything that your individual nature may require has ALREADY BEEN PROVIDED for you by the Creator. One has only to ACCEPT it, first in consciousness then in fact. Your STEADY RECOGNITION of this fact forms a veritable magnet in the mind which will attract every requirement to you, not as money that will drop in your lap without effort but as ideas, which when ACTED UPON, will yield an abundant harvest.

Try this. Begin right now to take the time, two or three times daily, to focus your thought at the base of the brain: "Spirit of God (Life), I AM GRATEFUL to you for the ABUNDANCE that IS mine now!" Any other good affirmation that may appeal to you, one that you compose for yourself perhaps, will do provided the use of it LIFTS your thought and feeling into CERTAINTY that abundance IS yours now. The more completely you can flood your mind, your CONSCIOUSNESS, with the recognition of Life's abundance, for you as well as for all, the more quickly your thought and feeling will manifest in FORM. Rich ideas will come to you intuitively, particularly if you impress the RICHES that ARE yours NOW upon your mind just before going to sleep. Any good idea if acted upon with wisdom and energy will yield great abundance for anyone who apprehends it and works in FAITH towards its fulfillment.

The Value of Sleep and a New Method of Inducing It:

Sleep is Nature's restorative for tired tissues and often is found to be the only effective refreshener of the body machine. The exact amount of sleep required varies with different individuals, much depending upon how fatigued a person is when retiring. If one feels the need of relaxation and sleep, and yet cannot easily go to sleep, try the following method, which you may have read in my book, "The Healing Power is Life." It is this: Sit nude on the edge of your bathtub, feet outside the tub. Take a fountain syringe and fill it with water that is blood-warm (NOT hot). Place the end of the tube at nape of neck and let the warm water trickle down your spine until you begin to feel relaxed; then go to bed quickly, comfortable, warm and relaxed.

Another aid towards relaxation (and relaxation, if complete, is sure to induce sleep in a weary person) is this: Lying in bed, on the back, deliberately send the message down to your toes, firmly, "Relax!" Continue sending the message until the toes do spread and relax. Then relax ankles in same manner, also knees, then base of spine, and the spine itself to base of head, also hands and arms. As a rule one will never get this far with the relaxation-exercise; almost invariably one will slip off into deep, restful sleep before having consciously relaxed more than half the body. Upon awakening if you feel recuperated, don't force yourself to remain in bed, whatever the hour.

Get up and do something that you are interested in doing. Be sure the room you sleep in is always well ventilated; almost all people breathe more deeply when sleeping than when awake, unless exercising quite freely. Do not eat a big meal just before retiring.

If you will give this method of inducing sleep a fair trial, you will find it very effective in inducing refreshing sleep that will have a real recuperative value.

11

"How To Live Life And Love It!"

MASTER: If you are anxious and uncertain about the future because of the fast-moving and extremely chaotic changes now going on all about you, here is a lesson that will help you find your true self and to stay at peace. Once we really find the true self we are in tune with Life as it is. Then we can live life and love it! Life really is glorious once one knows how to live it. Try to imagine for a few minutes that you know a secret which opens all of the closed doors of seeming limitation and that you can then step into a new world in which all is Life and Liberty. In order to enter this fair paradise of freedom the mind must be trained to choose carefully the emotional trend of thinking.

PUPIL: Do you mean that only those who have developed their different mental faculties through study and practice of Truth can enter this kingdom?

MASTER: That is exactly what I mean, since thoughts alone are creative. Those who have learned the value of the trained will, imagination, intuition, and who live accordingly, can really feel secure. The tendency of thought, the habits of thought, determine with precision one's outward affairs. So as you start to travel this road which leads to absolute liberty in all things it is necessary to leave behind all excess baggage such as self-pity, intolerance, criticism, fear, despondency, feelings of superiority, and all other negative and destructive occupants of your mental house. Take all these and put them in a secure bag; then tie a string of resolute determination tightly around them and dump them on a trash-pile. Cover the worthless bag of destructive evils with oil and set it on fire. Then are you really ready to start on your journey.

PUPIL: It would seem that one is only able to "go places" on this road by developing self-control. Is that so necessary?

MASTER: Yes, vitally necessary. However true and powerful a truth may be there must be a method of application of the principle to the individual. The best and surest method of manifesting the truth that God and man are one, and that God lives in and thinks through each of us, is to deliberately cultivate self-control with its consequent serenity of mind. In your endeavor to use this great Power for your individual purpose in the affairs of your hourly life you must be able to catch your thought the minute it begins to wander into doubts, fears, condemnations, criticisms, etc. and turn it in the direction you DO wish to go. Thus will you build certainty into your soul and body and the possession of certainty within means certainty and all things good in the affairs.

PUPIL: You make it seem that my disposition and self-control need much of my attention. I will admit that I am not patient; and of course I am intolerant, but only with those who deserve it -only with those who do not seem to try to do their part do I lose my temper.

MASTER: It is not my intention to be personal about your disposition. But I do say earnestly that every person who wishes to enjoy the blessings of true freedom MUST learn careful thought-selection, which means absolute thought-control, or self-control. In this way you will very soon entertain only the thought-guests you admire and enjoy. The uncouth, the grouchy, the selfish, the condemnatory, the suspicious, the tramp thoughts, all of whom will try to make a convenience of your mental domain, must be turned out of your mind. The best way to do this is put your whole feeling into an affirmation, whatever one appeals to you at the moment. Hold steadily to that thought and feeling until everything unlike it is out of your mind. Then lock your mental doors and use your will to keep out thoughts you have dismissed from your presence.

PUPIL: This making my mind do my new will is not going to be easy. I will practically have to make over completely my habitual mental processes.

MASTER: No, it will not be easy. But the goal the discipline will lead you to is worth a thousand times the effort required, however much effort that may be. If you will mentally stick tight to your resolve to make your mind a conscious center of divine operation, even for one week, seeing yourself growing steadily into what you wish to become, you will be amazed at your own growth and the genuine interest you have in everything around you.

Also you will discover many, many wonderful things about yourself that you never knew before. Once you focus your attention and your intention on the Intelligent Life within you, and try to reproduce it in your own self, you will begin to get results that will seem almost phenomenal to you, and at once. Keep your consciousness focused on the fact that the Spirit of Life has no fears, no anxiety, and soon your feeling will correspond with It. Just try this, say for two weeks, without slipping; then ask yourself if you would go back to your old estate, if you could.

PUPIL: Is one apt to be "hypnotized," and thus hindered in progress, by the thoughts of others about one? Sometimes I seem to be making real progress when suddenly, and for no apparent reason, there is an almost uncontrollable impulse and feeling of "oh what is the use!" I am like a ship without a rudder, trying to plow through some invisible, and invincible, force, and "getting nowhere fast," as the saying is. At best these experiences are long, long detours off the main road. What causes these episodes?

MASTER: You gave it its right name in the beginning. It is hypnotism; but as a rule it is self-hypnotism, almost unconsciously done because of the old habits of thought; and it comes as the result of your letting things other than your aim hold your attention. Your efforts to control your thoughts should be steady, continuous, with no unguarded moments. Mere spasmodic efforts, however strongly indulged in at the times of their occurrence to you, will never take you very far on the road to the new goal you have set. Before you study any further in these lessons, yes right now, make up your mind positively that you are entering upon the study to win, and that you will make an earnest, steady, continuous effort to do so.

My own personal remedy for overcoming any tendency to slip back into the old rut of wrong thinking, and I assure you that I have always found it a most potent and sure panacea, is, believe it or not, that wonderful thing, derisively called "old-fashioned and out of date" by some, -The Lord's Prayer. Go carefully over the Lord's Prayer every day. If you do not already know it thoroughly, memorize it, so that you can repeat it anywhere, anytime, silently if you like. Us it, repeat it carefully, slowly, and with much depth of feeling, as often as there is the least tendency to slip off your path.

After you have finished with your reading, or repetition of the Prayer, then take up your mental picture again, mentally seeing, feeling, believing, knowing that you are already in possession of whatever it is that you want.

This is what Jesus meant when He said for us to always, "ask believing that ye already have and ye SHALL HAVE!" If you will do these things, very soon you will find that you ARE on the road to Freedom and Joy, and it will constantly grow easier for you to stay on the highway, without so many detours.

PUPIL: Just now I should like very much to have more money. In fact I must have it. Do you mean that I can attract the money I need by living with the Lord's Prayer for, say half an hour every morning and every night, just "precipitate" the money right out of the very air? That seems incredible!

MASTER: What you ask is incredible! And you are not getting my real meaning. The finest statement of the Law of Life ever uttered is, in my opinion, that wonderful, wonderful statement of Jesus, namely: "Seek ye FIRST the kingdom of God and His righteousness (right-use-ness) and (then) all things will be added unto you." But please note that FIRST you must seek the kingdom, must make an honest effort to make your mind a center of divine operation only, and for its own sake and not from any ulterior motive.

Then will all things be added unto you. What happens to you through the steady, persistent use of the Lord's Prayer, as we were discussing it, is this: With the constant change in your mental attitude as you progress you are developing more and more strength and spiritual power. This self-mastery you are steadily developing is the growth of Divine Wisdom, Power and Beauty within you. Naturally then your whole outside world will gradually change to correspond to your new inside world because your most habitual thought takes outward form. Delightful changes will come into the circle of your individual world. Your thought and feeling will attract corresponding shapes; and you will feel much encouraged to go on and on and on into more and more joy and freedom.

12

Imagination And Intuition

MASTER: Today we shall discuss that great power we call imagination.

PUPIL: May I ask just what imagination is. I have heard you often speak of it as our "spiritual aeroplane," and say that "it wings us." But just what is it?

MASTER: No mortal can possibly answer that question. With all of our scientific research no one has found any rational clue as to the source of this great power, outside of God or Spirit. Nor has anyone been able to determine how far the use of imagination is able to carry one. It is Infinite. It is the mystery of mysteries; and it might be compared to electricity in this respect. Yet we know it does exist and that its power for good is inconceivable, if used constructively, correctly. What we should do is to inquire into its usefulness to us. Every normal person is equipped with it to some degree; and like the will the imagination can be developed. If rightly understood and correctly used it will perform seeming miracles.

PUPIL: But why do you call imagination the "spiritual aeroplane?"

MASTER: Because imagination, correctly used, can and will lift one, as if on wings, above and beyond all limitation, above one's low, narrow views of life, into a cloudless domain of true perspective. Imagination gives one clear vision of possibilities in your life which you have never been able to see before. Then while you realize that it takes determination and effort to achieve success; you also know that you can, with the imagination, tap the source of unlimited possibilities and Intelligent Energy. In a flash that mysterious, winged thing called imagination shows you where all the riches of Life are to be found.

PUPIL: Suppose one feels weak, obscure, poor, that you know your ideas are good but that you lack the money or health to carry them into effect. What can imagination do about these things?

MASTER: Imagination will reveal that strength and power and means are to be found within your Divine self and that a better and better acquaintance with, and a more frequent use of, the God-powers within is certain to lead to success on any line.

PUPIL: Can imagination lift one to great spiritual heights? Or does it pertain more to material success?

MASTER: Jesus, the Nazarene, lifted himself to the exalted Christhood through understanding and using his powers of imagination. Is that not reaching the heights spiritually?

PUPIL: Is it the imagination that opens the door for limitless good to enter?

MASTER: No, not correctly speaking. It is intuition, a feminine, or soul, quality which first captures an idea from the Infinite and passes it on to the imagination. Imagination raises one to a place in consciousness where all things are not only possible but are present, spiritual facts. Look all about at the ones who have risen above every conceivable handicap to very great success. Let us take Louis Pasteur, for example. He did not have any better mentality, or more strength, or more money, than any other ordinary Frenchman; and he was just as obscure as the lowest of them. His mental tools, by nature, were no sharper than yours are. But that strange and mysterious thing called imagination was very active in him and soared far beyond his scant equipment and early hardships into new realms of wisdom.

Many times he was not sure; but he imagined; and because he imagined he discovered; and because he discovered he wrought miraculous cures and to this day his wisdom prevents disease and death in countless millions. Truly Pasteur was a saint. The same is true of Paracelsus. People said he was lucky. Envious and lazy people always say this of anyone that succeeds. But the cures of Paracelsus were not luck; they were the result of his imagination and industry. Jesus intimately acquainted himself with God through the use of his fertile imagination; and through use of the same mystic power he was able to enter into other lives. His success easily can be attributed to his ability to see God (which is Perfection) in every person he contacted, however tragic, lonely, hopeless or vicious that one seemed. Through his recognition of God in all men he helped men to see God in themselves. This was the source of his great power!

PUPIL: Then imagination is a veritable dynamo and not just a means of trivial, idle day-dreaming?

MASTER: Yes. Recognize your imagination as a dynamo of limitless power. Use all of it that you possess whenever you need it. Understanding of it, and experience in using it, will readily prove it to be the most powerful force in your mental equipment. Used correctly it will carry your light up among the brightest stars of highest heaven. It is not enough to dream and idly desire, not any more than it is enough to start an aeroplane's motor just to watch the propeller go round and round. You must fuel your imagination with knowledge and purpose. You must take your bearings and hold your course. Risks, hardships, will be only still greater opportunities to use your imagination in your journey through the clouds.

PUPIL: All of this sounds very interesting and inspiring. But when I look about me and see the people who are succeeding, and who have so much more in life than I have, it is confusing. They do not seem to know, or care, a thing about God. How about that?

MASTER: If I were you I would try attending to my own knitting and start at once to develop my own power; also I would stop envying others their success.

PUPIL: Oh I am not envying anybody anything. I simply do not understand.

MASTER: It would help if you would try to avoid a tailspin of self-pity. As soon as you observe someone who is getting on better than you are you must project yourself into his life critically. Try doing this same thing constructively. Explore his tactics, his tastes, his imagination and industry; and then ask yourself if you might not get along better and faster if you adopted some of the means he employs.

PUPIL: How can I know how another does his work to succeed? And I did not realize that I have been feeling sorry for myself. How would it be to try to see myself as others see me?

MASTER: It would help very much if you will turn your imagination on yourself without any excuses or alibis. Your imagination will show you your true self if you have the courage to use it and trust it. And let you intuition help you also.

13

Husbands, Wives, Children

(Children, How to Bring Them Forth If You Wish Them, Home, Husbands, Wives, if You Desire Them.)

PUPIL: It seems to me that many of my married friends would be perfectly happy if only children would come to them. It seems strange they can not have any.

MASTER: No, it is not strange. It is all according to Law. "Principle is not governed by precedent." Children are the result of knowing, feeling, living that Law consciously or unconsciously; they are the birth of new ideas, something different. Every baby is a new idea, a new form in which Life lives. Get into the habit of developing new ideas and you will find these very ideas taking the form of children. It need not matter what the new ideas are about so long as you fully develop them. Then mentally picture as many children as you would like to have. When about to give birth to the new idea in form (a baby) I would suggest the daily help of a really good Mental Science practitioner, also at the time of birth. With proper understanding the birth of the child will be as natural as the spiritual idea which preceded the form.

PUPIL: All of this sounds very wonderful and convincing while I talk with you. At the risk of your thinking my mind a sieve may I ask you to put all three steps, husband, home, children, into concise, separate form.

MASTER: Very well. The idea of concentration is not a leaky one and I shall be happy to present them in the order you name. But first what, exactly what, does the word husband mean to you? What characteristics do you wish the husband to manifest? What should his disposition be in order to be in tune with yours? These are your very first steps along the way.

PUPIL: To me husband symbolizes certain characteristics I would like to attract to myself from the masculine side of Life, or quality of Life, a type of man I admire. His main qualities should be, for me, understanding and love. With these two attributes well-developed in both of us I believe happiness would be certain to follow.

MASTER: With love and understanding well developed in husband and wife happiness is certain to follow. The one certain way to attract this type of husband is to develop love and understanding in yourself. It is a very great truth that like attracts like! So first think over carefully just the type of man you feel could be happy with you.

PUPIL: Oh, I thought I was to think of the qualities my husband should have to make me happy.

MASTER: That method would help to develop self-centeredness, selfishness. But the other way is a reaching out to GIVE what you have and has a very great attracting power. When you have determined the type of man whom you feel would be happy with you, then take for yourself an early morning-hour and through reading and meditation think yourself into the quality of Life you wish to attract and hold the feeling. Herein lies the real value of holding your thought and feeling into place, just like plugging into the light socket when you want light. If you keep pulling the plug you will not get much light. The secret is: MAKE your contact in thought and feeling and HOLD IT, with a happy, expectant attitude. Of course this ability to hold an idea is arrived at by developing the will.

PUPIL: It seems to me that visualizing will not work unless the mental pictures made are held in place in mind. Is that right?

MASTER: That is exactly right. They must be held in place, again just like the electric contact for lights must be held in place if you are to benefit by the light which will then stay on. Your magnet of thought and feeling draws from out of the whole Universe such qualities as Love, Understanding, Protection, Provision, husband, children, whatever it is you have visualized.

PUPIL: It is like a postage-stamp then; it only has value if it sticks. Am I right about this: that what I really AM that I ATTRACT? Might this not be the meaning of Jesus' statement in Matthew 13:20 when he said "For whomsoever hath to him shall be given and he shall have more abundance; but whosoever hath not from him shall be taken away even that which he hath?" When one really HAS a husband in feeling and mentally pictures him one really does HAVE that husband; and he is SURE to appear in form as a human being: Is this not having more abundance? How slowly I grow. First I wanted my husband to have understanding; now I see that he IS understanding.

MASTER: That is it. Every conceivable thing that the human mind and heart can desire IS already in existence. Like the electricity it has always been there; and as soon as one realizes it and tunes the desire in with that quality of Life which it is the current begins to flow in that direction. Then one has real abundance through continually having the recognition that whatsoever he may want he already has it.

PUPIL: Is the process the same if one wants several children?

MASTER: Yes, fundamentally it is the same. If we wish to manifest our new ideas of Life in the form of children, it is necessary to make the desire known to God, the Great, Ever-Present, Formative, Responsive, Creative, Intelligent Power. It being Responsive and Creative it manifests in form, as children.

PUPIL: Just what should one first begin to think and feel?

MASTER: First, let us suppose that your desire for children is in perfect accord with the Divine Plan to bring into earth existence a continual advancement of the human race. So your idea of the new birth is that you may be a means, or a channel, through which the All-Creating Principle of Intelligent, Beautiful, Perfect Life may reproduce Itself in a new form, one capable of recognizing itself as an individualized action of Pure Spirit. Then by reading good articles or books or by meditating on an affirmation that appeals to you, you tune your thought and feeling in with the very highest rate of vibration.

Stay with the thought and feeling until you are certain that you HAVE made your contact with the Divine Intelligence, just as you are certain that you shall turn on the light when you plug into a light-socket. You know, under the latter circumstance, that the contact IS made because the room is flooded with light. And in the mental instance you know your contact IS made because your whole feeling IS flooded with certainty and a sense of security in God's Love and Power as they manifest in and through you.

PUPIL: It seems to me that one would have to keep constantly in mind the thought of begetting perfect ideas relative to every act.

MASTER: Jesus said: "Watch and pray lest you enter into temptation." You feel towards God (Life) in the same way your child feels toward you. If you obey the Laws of Life because you love your Father (Life) your child will do the same.

PUPIL: Is it necessary that both father and mother should desire the children? Should they take their meditations together? Should they discuss the hope of children?

MASTER: If both father and mother desire children the new idea will be a more perfect idea of God. It is not necessary to take the meditations together; in fact, I personally prefer to have all of my meditations alone. And it seems to me the less one discusses a desire with anyone the more quickly and perfectly the desire manifests. If one talks about a thing usually it is put in the future and is rarely discussed as a PRESENT FACT; hence the manifestation is delayed indefinitely because of the habit of looking upon it as a future manifestation, as something that "will be" rather than something that IS.

PUPIL: How is this for a method of bringing children of your own into one's personal life? First, study and think over the fundamental Law of Life as always giving expression to its highest ideals and ideas in human form. Man is God's highest ideal and the children of men are specialized ideas of the One Great Creative Source of all things. Are not our children the results of God's ideas of giving birth to our highest desires?

MASTER: You have the right idea. Try to really feel that God, Life, Love, Wisdom, is giving birth to a particular idea through you. Plant that idea, that thought-seed, in the garden of your individual subconscious mind. By using your individual subconscious quality of mind in this way you are doing your part to let all the Creative Energy in the Universe act in and through you without limit.

Thus you are a bridge between the two extremes in the scale of Nature, one of which is the innermost Creative Spirit of Life and the other the particular, external form of a child. Your objective quality of thought-power mentally sees your perfect child, then passes the thought and the picture into the creative power of your individual quality of subconscious mind which in turn transfers the thought-seed into ALL of the growing power there is in Life, thus bridging the two extremes of Nature. Your thought-seed will grow into perfect externalization just as a kernel of corn will when planted under the proper conditions.

PUPIL: This idea of a thought-seed clears up the whole Idea that my individual subconscious mind is the bridge between myself and the whole vast sea of Life.

MASTER: If you plant a kernel of corn you first make sure the soil and the climate is the proper kind to grow corn.

PUPIL: Does that mean I should look into my own character and physical condition, and so forth, to determine if I really am the type of woman to bear perfect children?

MASTER: You are right. It is vitally important to know these things. Once you have found out that these are clear, and you and your husband are sure in your minds that you wish to create in form your highest ideal of Love, as children, then proceed. Remember that the seed you plant, having all the vitality, all the vital essence, necessary to draw to itself from out of All Life every element necessary to cause it to grow into a perfect outward reproduction, a perfect child.

Every parent, or parent-to-be, should be an enlightened parent, of course, and should do all within the power to bring forth, cherish, nurture and rear, the finest children possible. It will help those who are, or who desire to be, parents if they will inform themselves fully along the most scientific lines on this question. This they may do in numerous ways, through the reading of good books on the subject, ones that are written by specialists, also by taking courses on the subject that are offered almost continually through university extension plans, also in many places by city and state departments; and lastly to seek the advice and care of the best physicians from conception forward.

14

Life, Love, Beauty

MASTER: In his wonderful books Judge Troward stresses often that the Spirit of Life also is one of Love and Beauty, and that where the One is the others will be found, too, as a matter of necessity. Where Life is Love is. One is the correlative of the other. Where Life and Love are Beauty must be.

PUPIL: May we have another illustration to clarify this?

MASTER: Certainly. All persons have an appreciation of art. The ancient Greeks were supreme in the arts for many centuries. To this day many of their works have never been equaled. I have never seen that fact more compellingly illustrated than it was one day last summer at our home on The Esplanade, Redondo Beach, California. A gentleman friend of Mr. Smith's (Worth Smith, my husband) who, like Mr. Smith, has been a student of the Great Pyramid for many years, called on us. He brought a wonderful book and showed us many lovely pictures of exquisite Greek vases. Alongside each photograph was a sketch of the same vase with the basic design highlighted in geometry, many lines drawn to salient features of the sketch.

Of all the grace and beauty and absolute perfection of symmetry I have ever seen, or hope to, those pictures and sketches had it, without a solitary flaw in any of them. Each was purest harmony, so much so that one marveled and it seemed that music itself flowed from them. Each vase was an expression of God and His laws of Life, Love, Beauty and Harmony, executed to perfection by artists in whom His Love, Beauty, Harmony LIVED. Because of their adoration of Beauty, and its Source in the Father, they were able to conceive Beauty in the mind when planning the designs of the vases. No doubt they sketched the designs as shown in the book, by employment of the geometry in which they excelled. With the model before them they then fashioned the works of superb Harmony to glorify the earth. Wherever perfect Harmony is there you will find perfect Love for they are twin blessings!

PUPIL: But all of us can not make such masterpieces, you know, for all of us do not have such artistic talents. Do we?

MASTER: All of us have some talent within us. Unfortunately, many seem to never realize it and never do anything about it. Even so any person of intelligence can put into whatever task that one may have to do the Spirit of Life, Love, Beauty and Harmony, IF only one will, and can make of the fruits of the task many things of Beauty. Some housewives, for example, make of housekeeping and rearing children a thing of drudgery as a result of their lack of illumination about the true divinity of housekeeping. Others put Love, Beauty, Harmony, Order and Joy into the same task and make a glory of it. It is a matter of the spiritual consciousness one has, or acquires through study if it is not there innately .

PUPIL: Will you please cite an example from the Bible which features this matter of consciousness of our divinity as being the root of all blessings?

MASTER: Gladly indeed. Study carefully St. Matthew, chapter 13, verse 12. Jesus uttered those golden words to teach mankind that like does attract like, INvariably and INfallibly. That passage states the law of attraction at its best, including an unshakable faith, visualizing by means of which one HAS spiritually, or in the mind, even that which is sought, and which serves as a magnet of infinite power to draw to one the glad fulfillment in form, or physical reality, provided only one also WORKS confidently and happily to carry out the ideas the Father gives one, through intuition, as steps in the path to the shining goal.

Now let us directly quote the passage, then strip it bare of all the "mystery" so many claim it contains for them. Unfortunately, to many that verse remains a riddle for life unless they are sufficiently interested to seek until they find the key to its solution. The passage reads:

"For whosoever HATH, to him shall be given, and he shall have more abundance: but whosoever hath NOT from him shall be taken away even that he hath."

The big question is: "For whosoever hath" what? Does it mean the one who has wealth of money, or property, or other earthly possessions? No, although the one who has the thing that is meant is certain to acquire financial independence and retain it. It means simply that "whosoever hath" the CONSCIOUSNESS of the Father within, who has that exalted awareness as an abiding conviction, who has implicit faith in it, and who actively carries on in the work that one does, whatever it may be, the ideas of Life, Love, Beauty and Harmony the Father gives that one in an UNending stream, to that one will be GIVEN ALL he may ever require, and to spare. But the person who "hath not" the high consciousness is subject to all the sorrows, lacks and other inharmonies circumstances and conditions can bring to bear upon him, even to the point of losing all he has gained through habitual employment of secondary causation. . . for since he has not the awareness he is, or shall be, "under the rule of an iron destiny," to quote Troward, and dwells in anxiety and fear, knowing not that "the eternal God is our refuge and a very present help in trouble."

PUPIL: Can that Love, Beauty and Harmony be caused to flow from one person, a practitioner let us say, into and through another so that the second party will be aware of the spiritual uplift, and receive corresponding benefits?

MASTER: Yes, indeed, that is done easily. That is the mission of the practitioner, for he or she does these things for others many hours a day. I well recall an incident that occurred not long ago in the beautiful home of a dearly beloved friend and student in Denver. I was sitting with her privately in her lovely living-room, holding her left hand in my right, thus completing a circuit exactly as an electric circuit is made, positive pole in contact with the negative pole. With my mind I made contact with the Love, Beauty and Harmony the Spirit is. From the Universal Spirit of Life those qualities flowed into me, and through me into my dear friend, and through her back into the Universal. For minutes we kept the contact and both of us were aware of the surge of tremendous power flowing through us. I have this friend's kind permission to mention her name. She is Grace N. Northcutt. It is she whose gracious generosity accounts for the new edition of this book you are now reading.

PUPIL: Then it is true that as one makes of it a habit to consciously recognize God in one's daily, hourly, even minute-by-minute living in that degree one will get good results?

MASTER: Yes. The correspondence is exact! As we apply the laws of electricity we are certain to get results that correspond to those laws only. It is folly to apply one set of creative laws to a problem and expect to get results that correspond to a different code. So it is that if we set in motion through concentrated and consecrated thinking the laws of Harmony then only Harmony will manifest in and through us, and in our affairs!

Again I give you the golden key which will unlock any door of bondage and which will never disappoint you if you persist in the use of it in wisdom. It is, I repeat, that twelfth verse of the thirteen chapter of Matthew.

PUPIL: How is it obtained? What price does one have to pay for the key?

MASTER: The price is given in the fifteenth chapter of John and is, as Jesus said: "ABIDE IN ME!" That will put you in an entirely new relationship to your Father and to your environment, will open up many new possibilities hitherto undreamed of, all by an orderly sequence of creative laws that result from your new mental attitude. Thought is the energy by which the law of attraction is brought into operation. It is by thought that we keep the sap of life flowing from the trunk into the branches. The statement Jesus made in Matthew 13:12 is so important that He made it repeatedly, worded a bit differently, yet containing the self-same law He expressed therein.

PUPIL: May we have a schedule, and some affirmations, for daily use? If we have one before us, in print, it should help a lot, it seems to me, in our follow-through.

MASTER: First I shall give you two affirmations I have found very effective and powerful when consistently used with profound feeling.

1. "Father, I thank Thee for the conscious knowledge that all my good comes from Thee only, and that I no longer look to man as the source of my supply!"

2. "God IS my ever-present supply and large sums of money come to me quickly, under grace and in perfect ways, so to bountifully supply my every need, and to spare!"

Moreover a careful study of these three references will be a great aid, i.e., Mark 5:36 and 9:23, John 20:29.

Lastly, I am happy to give you an excellent routine for daily use that Troward himself gave to me. I have used it faithfully for thirty-five years now and it is a powerful help indeed.

It is this:

MONDAY. . . Watch your words!

TUESDAY. . . Watch your feeling!

WEDNESDAY. . . Watch your acts!

THURSDAY. . . Watch your receiving!

FRIDAY. . . Watch your giving!

SATURDAY. . . Look for the Spirit of Life and Love in everybody and in everything!

SUNDAY. . . Let the Lord's Prayer abide with you continually!

THE END

Printed in Great Britain
by Amazon